The ART

of

WAR

FOR THE NEW MILLENNIUM

DAN LOK AND SUN TSU

An Imprint of Morgan James Publishing, LLC

NEW YORK

THE ART OF WAR FOR THE NEW MILLENIUM
© 2006 Dan Lok. All rights reserved.

ISBN: 1-933596-57-0 (Paperback)

Published by:

Knowledge Exchange Press
An Imprint of Morgan James Publishing, LLC
1225 Franklin Ave Ste 325
Garden City, NY 11530-1693
Toll Free 800-485-4943
www.MorganJamesPublishing.com

Habitat for Humanity®
Peninsula
Building Partner

Cover and Interior Design by:
Tony Laidig
www.thecoverexpert.com
tony@thecoverexpert.com

TABLE OF CONTENTS

iii

V

ix

Introduction

THE 14-YEAR OLD BUSINESS WARRIOR

My father gave me the Chinese version of "The Art of War" when I was 14 years old. He said, "This book contains some of the greatest wisdom in the world. You must read it. If you truly understand and digest what Sun Tzu's work, then you'll succeed in business beyond your wildest dreams…and you'll appreciate what a genius Sun Tzu is."

Looking back, the book had a huge impact in my life. There are two books that had a huge positive influence in my life, and "The Art of War" is one of them.

I am successful today is because I applied the strategies…

That's why I want to bring this book to you. That's why I've revised it and make it more user-friendly. That's why I've put a lot of effort into making it more applicable to today's business world.

I wanted to make it more like a business how-to book instead a military philosophy book because I believe we can all benefit from the wisdom of Sun Tsu.

There are many different versions of The Art of War. I don't claim that this is the BEST version, but I DO believe it is the MOST PRACTICAL version. I've added my personal spin and combined some of the strategies with my own experience… and included action steps so that you can start applying these strategies

If you've ever tried to read Sun Tzu's "The Art of War," you probably gave up halfway through it. And that's a real shame, because "The Art of War" is like the old "girl with a great personality."

You know the one I mean: the girl who's funny, smart, honest, and caring…but her looks are only so-so. Most guys don't take the time to get to know her because they make decisions based on looks. But for the guy who's willing to invest the time in getting to know the girl with the great personality, the rewards can be rich.

Sure, there are other business books out there that claim to teach you everything you need to know about marketing and influence. They've got sexy covers and catchy titles. Unfortunately, most of them are like beautiful girls who look good, but can't hold an intelligent conversation for five minutes.

"The Art of War" is like the girl with the great personality. It's hard to get to know. It's cryptic. Some of the phrasing is dated (yeah, go figure—it was written in about 500 B.C, some 2,500 years ago.) To learn the valuable lessons it teaches, you have to study ancient Chinese warfare first, and that takes time…time that no one seems to have to spare in the 21st century.

So I've done the heavy lifting for you. This book takes all the relevant lessons of the Samurai and translates them into modern life lessons that you can use to amp up your marketing.

Why study these lessons? Because of a guy I once worked with. His name was Jack. I always used to wonder why companies love to hire people with military experience. Cynically, I figured it had something to do with politics. Then I met Jack.

Jack was the manager in charge of marketing for the software development company I worked at. He was a crew-cut ex-Marine, early 40's, and on his desk he kept a beaten-up, dog-eared copy of "The Art of War." I never paid that book much attention…until the thing happened with the two interns.

Six college interns had been hired to implement our marketing strategy. After their orientation, Jack gave two of them, Mary Sue and Pete, their first assignment. "Here's a list of local companies that use our competitors' software," he told them. "Organize your fellow interns into a team, call these companies up, ask to speak with the lead database developer, and then go over these talking points with them to sell them our database software."

Mary Sue glanced at Pete, he glanced back, and they both grinned, as if this was all just a big joke. I had a bad feeling about that, but I didn't say anything.

At the end of the week, Jack walked over to the cubical that Pete and Mary Sue shared with the other interns. "So how many calls did you make, and how many software licenses did you sell?" he asked.

Again, they looked at each other and grinned, and I wondered if this was annoying Jack as much as me. Pete spoke up. "Well, we made a few calls on Monday, but mostly got voice-mail, so we decided to switch to e-mail."

"I see," Jack replied. "And how many licenses have you sold?"

Mary shifted uncomfortably. "Well, we sent out, like, about a hundred e-mails, so we're hoping we'll hear back from some people next week…"

"So the answer is 'none'?"

"Well, none so far," Pete hedged.

Jack frowned. "Perhaps I wasn't clear. E-mail marketing is too easy to ignore. I want you to call them on the phone. If you get voice-mail, leave a message and follow up with another phone call the next day. You may send an e-mail along with your follow-up call, but your first method of contact should always be a phone call."

Again, the glance and the giggle.

Jack ignored the response. He was more diplomatic than I would have been. "Next week, I want you to call every company on your list again and do what I just told you."

A week passed. I didn't see the interns using the phone much, except for personal calls, so I was curious to see what would happen on Friday.

Late Friday afternoon, Jack showed up at the interns' cube again. "Did you call them all?" he asked, short and to the point.

Pete responded, "Uh, actually, Mary Sue and I had a meeting, and we decided that what we really needed to do was refine our e-mail strategy, so we spent two days doing that, and then everyone pitched in and helped us put together a killer e-mail sales letter with some really cool graphics, and—"

Jack cut him off. "So you didn't make any calls?"

"Ah, no, we—"

"Pete, Mary Sue...you're fired."

As Pete and Mary Sue sat their with their mouths hanging wide open, Jack instructed the remaining four interns to make those calls on Monday—all of them.

On Monday afternoon, Jack returned to the interns' cube. "Made the calls?" he asked the interns. Four heads bobbed up and down quickly, and one of the interns handed Jack the sheet with the company's names. Beside each name were dates, times, notes pertaining to the calls, the follow-ups, and the eventual conversations.

Better yet, the interns had sold twenty software licenses.

———

In most books written on the "The Art of War," you'll find a story called, "The Lesson of the Concubines." It's similar to what happened with the interns, only it deals with Chinese concubines.

After Sun Tzu wrote "The Art of War," the King of We, a guy named Ho Lu, heard about it and decided to test it out. Since he didn't want to lose valuable warriors, he tested it on some women from his palace, since women were seen as expendable back then.

Sun Tzu divided the 180 women up into two companies and put one of the king's favorite concubines at the head of each. If you're not familiar with the term "concubines," think: favorite kept woman, or just really good prostitute.

Long story short, Sun Tzu asked the girls if they knew what "front, "back", "left" and "right" meant. They said they did, so they were given spears and axes and the drill began.

Sun Tzu shouted, "Right turn!"

But the girls weren't taking this seriously, so they just giggled. It was all a big joke, right? Not quite…

Seeing the giggles, Sun Tzu declared, "If orders aren't clear, or if they're not understood, it's the general's fault. But if the orders are clear and the soldiers disobey anyway, then it's the officers' fault."

Then he ordered the two concubines beheaded.

When the king saw what was about to happen, he freaked. "Whoa dude," he said, "you don't need to go there! I get your point, and I know you can handle troops. If you kill my two best whores, the palace feasts just won't be the same. Don't do it!"

But Sun Tzu said, "No way. You put me in charge. Since I'm running the show here, I don't have to follow all your orders." And he had the two concubines beheaded. Then he promoted the next two highest-ranking women to lead each company and started a new drill.

This time, those women were all business. They turned left on command, then right, they marched ahead, they boogied on back...without a single smile or giggle. No doubt they were scared shitless, but they performed flawlessly.

Sun Tzu sent a message to the king, telling him that his women soldiers were now properly drilled and disciplined, and that they would go through hell and high water if they were ordered to.

The king's response was something along the lines of, "Yeah, I got that part. Cut the crap. The show's over."

Sun Tzu hollered back, "Your mouth writes checks you're afraid to cash!"

The king was pissed, but he had to admit that when it came to war, Sun Tzu was The Man. After he got over being pissed, he appointed Sun Tzu as general.

This little story about the tragic death of a couple of prostitutes illustrates an important point that we'll discuss in more detail later on. The old Chinese version goes like: "There are commands of the sovereign which must not be obeyed." The modern version is:

> Don't follow bogus orders

In the following chapters, I'll demystify "The Art of War" for you and show you, step-by-step, how you can use basic principles that have won countless wars over the last 2,500 years to improve that special form of warfare that we like to call business.

xvii

And in the chapter you're about to read, you'll learn how you can gain an instant edge over your competitors by using a few simple Chinese warfare tricks. Wanna know how it's done? I thought you would! Read on…

Chapter 1

KICK YOUR COMPETITION'S BUTT BY USING MILITARY PRINCIPLES IN BUSINESS

I n this chapter, I'm going to give you the basic toolbox you'll need to get the maximum mileage out of this incredible book. You're learn why these principles work, and how to take the ball and run with it after you read the tips I'm going to share with you.

We live in the touchy-feely Age of Nice. It begins on the soccer fields, where kids are rewarded with all kinds of decorative ribbons and trophies just for showing up and participating. Participating and encouraging others is what you're supposed to do. Adopting a hard-core competitive mindset is not. But which one do you think will take you farthest in business? Yep, you got it— that ugly old competitive spirit.

But modern American society frowns on being competitive. It's considered unseemly to bare your fangs, let your adrenaline roar, and do your damnedest to out-do the other guy or gal. In public schools and colleges, grades have become almost meaningless as teachers and administrators cater to an imagined fragile sense of self-esteem that they think their students have. Bet they'd be surprised to learn that 90% of their students are a lot tougher than they think!

Fortunately for you, many of your competitors have internalized the lessons learned in the politically correct schools and playgrounds of late 20th and early 21st century America. Why do I say that's good for you? Because they won't get down and dirty to beat your brains out in the business arena. If they even try, they'll feel so bad about it that they'll go back to networking with you and buying you Starbucks…even though you work for their competitor.

Here's a newsflash: business IS war. They're both zero-sum games. What does that mean? It means that there aren't too many win-win situations. If Company ABC competes against Company XYZ, for every $1 in that ABC gains in market-share, XYZ loses $1. The only way to have a win-win is to expand the market, which can be done, but then you're still fighting your competitors over the same pie—it's just a bigger pie.

2

And when you're in marketing, you're competing for the same customers. It works that way in war, too. Wars are fought for resources, be they land, oil, shipping lanes, or control of terrorism. In business you're fighting for the money that consumers are prepared to spend.

Let me put it plainly: if you spend all your time smiling, making happy-talk, and try to build consensus, you WILL get stomped in business by a competitor who's willing to use tried and true military tactics to grab customer dollars right out from under your nose. Who do you want to be, the nice guy who gets stomped, or the savvy guy who succeeds?

Yeah, that's what I thought. Want to succeed in business? Then read on, and you'll learn some incredibly useful things, such as what Sun Tzu has in common with Kenny Rodgers (they both advise you to know when to hold 'em and know when to fold 'em.)

The 5 Essentials for Victory:

1. Know when to fight and when not to fight.

2. Know how to handle both competent and incompetent people.

3. Have strong morale within your organization.

4. Be prepared so that you can take the competition by surprise when they aren't expecting it.

5. Be competent at what you do, and have a manager who supports your empowerment.

How to get more than your money's worth from this book

3

To make it easy and quick for you to learn, absorb and run with the lessons learned from this book, in each chapter we've presented the original text, preceded by our take on what this particular lesson means for you as a marketer and an executive of the 21st century warrior class. This way, it's easy for you to flip from the lesson to the original text to see how it relates.

In between the new text and the original, we've included some action steps for you to take so that you can immediately apply what you've learned.

Next, I'm going to let you in on a few secrets, like some of the screw-ups that the biggest corporations in American have made, and how they recovered. You'll learn some amazingly useful tactics for guerilla trench warfare on the battle ground we call modern American business.

Chapter 2

TAKE YOUR SALES TO THE NEXT LEVEL BY USING SECRETS OF ANCIENT CHINESE WARFARE

N ewsflash: AT&T was once royally nailed by the US government, all because of one big mistake. Want to know what it was, and how they recovered? Read on, and I'll tell you all about it…

One of the oldest cop-outs in the world consists of just four short words: "Maybe they won't come." This has been the basis for many a military and business blunder. It stems from a deep-seated human need for wish fulfillment; if we wish and hope that the enemy (and by enemy, I mean your competition in the marketplace) just won't show up, we don't have to prepare.

It's a lazy person's way of getting out of work. Don't yield to it. Think no one uses that excuse anymore? Think again. Let me transport you back to the year 1969…

How AT&T lost their 800-pound gorilla status

American Telephone and Telegraph (AT&T) and the Bell System the United States public network was the primary standard-setter for practices, procedures, and equipment in the fast-growing phone industry. Bell Labs, which is now owned by Lucent Technologies, was a hotbed of innovation, having to date generated 28,000 patents since it's inception in 1925.

But that was in the back part of AT&T/Bell's house. In the front parlor, things were much different...as many customers found out when they called the phone company for assistance.

Let's put it this way: the customer service at AT&T/Bell was such that it inspired Lilly Tomlin, on the comedy show "Laugh-In" (1968-1973), to create a character named Ernestine. Ernestine was a phone company operator, and whenever she got riles—which was often—her stock reply was, "We don't *have* to care...we're the *phone company!*"

Too bad Sun Tzu wasn't still around to advise AT&T/Bell. Here's what he would have said:

6

> Don't rely on the enemy not coming.
>
> Instead, rely on being ready.

AT&T/Bell was able to get away with treating customers any way they liked because, according to the U.S. Department of Justice (DOJ), they were a monopoly. But all good things come to an end. On November 20th, 1974, the DOJ filed suit, alleging anticompetitive behavior and seeking a breakup in the Bell System.[1]

On January 1st, 1984, the Bell System ceased to exist, with the exception of local markets such as Southwestern Bell in Texas, cumulatively known as "Baby Bells."

---

1. Souce: http://www.bellsystemmemorial.com

A stunned AT&T was now forced to compete for customers, a task which they performed badly at first, which added to budgetary woes that were already strained under the weight of legal bills. But the same company that produced the brilliant Bell Labs, a cauldron of creativity, did what they needed to do to save their company: they watched and listened.

As competitors sprung up, customers who'd been frustrated at the lack of choices rushed to sign up. Many of them were soon even more frustrated, because the newcomers lacked the technological expertise of AT&T. Customer service is useless without a product that works well to back it up.

However, many customers stayed with AT&T's new competitors, and AT&T made it their mission to find out why. The secret? Better customer service.

7

AT&T wised up, poured money and training into customer service, and it paid off to the extent that most people under 40 in America today think of AT&T as a company that provides good service based upon their experience with AT&T's now-defunct cell phone business.

Today, AT&T is trying to reassemble the organization they once had. And they could have kept it, had they only relied on their own readiness in dealing with customers, instead of counting on the fact that they were a monopoly and assuming that they always would be.

Never make the mistake of thinking that your competitor won't enter that new market you're getting into. Don't ever say things like:

- *"They've never marketed ring-tones before, so we don't have to worry about them."* Just watch them start when you start marketing ring-tones.

- *"We've got a clear field…no one else in the U.S. is in this market."* They soon will be once you light the way for them.

- *"We've got a patent on the process."* Patents have an expiration date. Too, it's not that difficult to reverse-engineer something, tweak it slightly so as to be different, and market it in a nearby niche.

Brainstorm with your marketing people on the "what if's", and then take a good, honest look at your underlying marketing assumptions. Is your strategy based on the competition not showing up? If so, you need to alter that assumption. Don't divert a lot of resources into contingency plans yet, but do make sure that you *have* contingency plans.

Solving the ultimate management headache— the Great Wall of China

You hear a lot about how the Great Wall of China was built. What you don't hear about is how it was manned and maintained, which is a shame because that system paved the way for all the on-site cappuccino bars, massage therapy, free cokes, gourmet lunches and more that you saw a lot of dot-bombs offering just before they all ran off a cliff in the late 1990's.

I'll explain.

The Great Wall was built as a barrier to the barbarian hordes that lay outside China, spoiling for a chance to bring down the

8

empire. It was also built as a monument to the union of China, which was achieved by Emperor Chin Hwang-ti circa 225 B.C.

The problem with building such a barrier was that it wasn't going to defend itself—men had to be trained and stationed all along it so that if the Barbarians got the notion to do something clever like come with a battering ram, the Chinese could fell them with arrows before it came to that.

But now the Emperor had a staffing problem. How could he convince tens of thousands of men to accept long tours of duty out on the literal edge of the empire, without their families or other comforts?

The solution: by convincing them to think of the Wall *as their home.* Instead of coming across as a hard-ass, the Emperor decided to get what he needed by being Mr. Nice Guy. Obviously, he'd heard the old saying about getting more ants with honey than with sugar.

He made a public announcement that any man of fighting age would be given a grant of land near the Wall, and certain other creature comforts. The way the offer was presented was more like a call for settlers than for warriors. The only catch was that pesky guard duty that had to be fulfilled as part of the deal. Guards were also encouraged to marry local girls who lived with their families near that section of the wall, which further cemented the guard's ties to his new community.

It worked brilliantly. When a guard wasn't on duty, he was out on his brand, spanking new land, cultivating crops, or visiting with his new wife's family.

There was just one little glitch…farming land takes a lot of time, as does being a good member of a community. And since

9

the Emperor was already granting the guards land, their actual pay wasn't anything great. In fact, it was so not-great that many guards moon-lighted, doing other work, and became more like peasants and laborers who occasionally pulled guard duty than like actual guards.

This lack of compelling loyalty ultimately did China in when famed Mongol Horde leader Genghis Khan (1162-1227) bribed a guard to let him—and his entire horde—through the gate.

But it was a nice idea, and one that Corporate America caught onto in the early 1990's. CEO's and stockholders were looking to increase productivity any way they could. Since employee benefits comprised 25 to 40% of base salary, the last thing they wanted to do was to hire more people. What they needed to do was find a way to convince employees to put in longer hours at work.

Most employees, though, resisted longer hours. So managers tried to make longer hours mandatory, and in doing so largely fell afoul of the Fair Labor Standards Act. In other words, the stick approach just wasn't going to work.

So they took a page from Emperor Hwang-ti's book and used the carrot approach—they made the work environment, as politically correct types call it, a nicer and much more hospitable place to be. Hot gourmet pasta stations and salad bars inside on-site cafeterias replaced dreary sandwich machines or "roach coaches", free sodas and coffee were put out in unlimited quantities, glittering chrome Wellness Centers were opened…and at the height of the dot-com boom, companies were even footing the tab for sending out employee's laundry and bringing in CPAs to do their taxes.

All of this was done to encourage employees to "settle" into the work place as if it were their home, and thus spend eighty or a hundred hours a week at the office.

Did it work? It did, for awhile. In particular, it worked well with employees who were unmarried and had no kids, and on foreign workers who came over to the US without their families, or, in other words, the entire software industry workforce.

But then the dot-com bust happened in early 2000. It made no difference how many different kinds of coffee companies had on tap for free if you didn't have a job anymore.

So how do you manage the Great Wall of China? By getting the people you need to manage it to look at it as their home.

Psst—people are spying on your infrastructure!

In ancient China, you could tell a lot about the character of the Emperor by the condition of the roads.[2] If the current Emperor was young, energetic, and ambitions, he would go order the roads and bridges to be repaired, maintained, and new ones built. On the other hand, Emperors who were lazy and unambitious, or who had a thin treasury, would let the roads fall apart.

Foreigners learned this early on, and a critical part of any reconnaissance mission was an assessment of the roads. If they were new and good, it probably wasn't a good ideal to try to conquer that juicy little border town.

What does this mean for you and your company's marketing? Well, if you're marketing B2B, one of the ways in which a company will size you up is by looking at your infrastructure. If

11

---

2. Source: Sun Tzu, "The Art of War", Dover edition, 2002, The Military Service Publishing Company, Harrisburg, Pennsylvania, ISBN 0-486-42557-6.

you're in an old, faded warehouse, your parking lot is potholed asphalt, and your receptionist acts less than happy to greet visitors, consider the message you're sending: *"We don't care about where we work, so why should we care about your business?"*

Infrastructure also means your people. Have you invested in training? Do they have the tools they need to do the job, or are they using software versions that went out with the Clinton Administration?

Maintain a good infrastructure, in terms of your physical work place and in terms of your people. It will give you the platform you need to achieve excellence, and besides…your customers will notice.

When you win, crush them like a bug

When you achieve a victory, you must follow it up.

In 1991, in response to Iraq's invasion of Kuwait in late 1990, the US invaded Iraq. The Gulf War lasted about six weeks, and ended with a cease-fire. In a decision that remains controversial, President Bush the Elder (the father, not the son) decided not to send US forces into Baghdad in pursuit of Saddam Hussein.

President Reagan had made a similar decision when, minutes after he took office, 52 hostages held in Tehran, Iran were released after being held for 444 days. The real work of their release was secured by President Carter, who agreed to pay off the Iranian militants. Reagan celebrated the release as a victory and did not follow it up.

In 2003, Saddam Hussein remained alive and well in Iraq and the US—for reasons that remain controversial—went into Iraq again, this time finally capturing Hussein.

My least politically-correct friend describes the situation with Iran and Iraq this way: "If we would have just nuked the living daylights out of both of 'em back in 1979, we'd have saved ourselves a good 25 years of nothing but trouble." Of course, we'd probably have started new wars, but she does have a point.

> Don't take half-measures.
>
> Always follow up a victory.
>
> Don't give the competition time to recover.

I know it sounds cruel and heartless, but when you've got your competitor on the ropes, finish him off. Never wound him badly then leave him alive—and, of course, I'm speaking metaphorically. What I mean is, if you take market-share away, *keep* it away. Have a meeting with your team and decide what you need to do to maintain your new customers.

Gain the power of having the facts on your side

One of the worst mistakes you can make is charging blindly ahead, without gathering complete information. I'm not saying you need to know every little thing, to the point that you get bogged down with analysis paralysis. What I mean is, decide what you need to know going in, then make sure you have that information.

Remember New Coke? In 1985, the Coca-Cola company was in a bad spot. The number of people who were moving away from sugary sodas was growing. These people were shifting to juices, exotic coffees, teas, bottled water…anything but sodas.

13

And then there was the Pepsi threat. Pepsi was already beating Coke in blind taste-tests (the "Pepsi Challenge"), and it was only a matter of time before Pepsi outsold Coke, at the rate Pepsi was gaining.

After many desperate brainstorming sessions, the Coke gurus decided that since Diet Coke was gaining in popularity, the best thing to do would be to create a new Coke by stripping the artificial sweeteners out of Diet Coke, adding back high-fructose corn syrup, and marketing the dickens out of it. After all, Diet Coke was already pretty darn close to Pepsi in taste...

Since they didn't want Pepsi to gain the cola crown just because Coca-Cola's fans were split between the original and the new, they discontinued the original. And in an amazing burst of marketing creativity, they named it...New Coke.

14

The information they *neglected* to gather? They didn't bother to ask anyone, point-blank, what they would think about Coca-Cola dropping the cola that they had made into an American icon through decades of careful marketing. They relied on blind taste-tests, all of which favored Pepsi. They figured people were ready for New Coke.

They were wrong.

The screams and wails of outrage began about five minutes after New Coke hit the shelves and the original was yanked. Even people who drank very little Coke howled with an emotional fervor that amazed Coca-Cola. It turned out that even people who didn't drink Coke had an emotional attachment to what they saw as a true-blue American classic and they *did not appreciate anyone messing with it.*

After three months of angry letters and phone calls, Coca-Cola relented and brought back the original under the label "Coca-Cola Classic." It sold like the proverbial hotcakes, and even after the initial excitement settled down, sales retained some of the boost. And the 3% of Coke drinkers who'd actually liked New Coke gravitated to Diet Coke.[3] (It may have been this whole fiasco that spawned the invention of the focus group, in which real people are actually asked what they think.)

Learn this lesson: when you plan a campaign, first find out *what* you need to know, then get that information.

Gain peace by fighting for it

If you want peace, you must fight for it. You can't buy it.

Around the turn of the second millennium (circa 1,000 a.d.), the Tatars, who were Turkish people in eastern Europe and central Asia, were making trouble for China. This was nothing especially new; the Tatars had been trouble for hundreds of years. But this time was to be different, for Emperor Chintsong was in charge of China.

Chintsong was not what you could call an iron man with cajones of steel. He was more of a Silly-Putty guy with cajones of pudding. When the Tatars conducted raids, Emperor Chintsong did the obligatory Emperor thing and mustered up a large army to meet the Tatars. That part, he got right. The rest, not so good.

When the two armies came face to face, Chintsong lost his nerve and allowed himself to be persuaded to pay the Tatars an annual allowance of silk and money in return for the Tatars giving

15

3. Source: http://www.snopes.com/cokelore/newcoke.asp

up several captured towns and promising not to raid Chinese territory again.[4] Instead of ensuring peace by fighting for it, the Emperor chose to try to buy peace.

Later, the Tatars reneged on the deal, conquered all of China, and founded the Manchu dynasty. All because one Emperor chose to spend instead of fight.

Flash forward to the modern world. In 2005, the state of Israel gave up the Gaza strip, ordering Jewish settlers out and even extracting some of them by force. The thinking was that if Israel gave up land to the Palestinians, they could buy peace. Within months, the Palestinians were using their newly-acquired premises to launch rocket attacks into Israel. Some people never learn…

The most common modern equivalent of trying to buy peace is driven by the need to be liked. Too many people these days will cave in and give their enemy what they want just to be liked. When this occurs on a verbal level, it's called "political correctness." Don't fall for it.

If you buy peace, you will be seen as weak.

If you want peace, fight for it.

You're mastered quite a bit of new information in the past few pages. Are you ready for the next chapter? I hope so. In it, you're going to discover how to plan better campaigns that result in bigger cash profits from every ad, postcard, sales letter and web page you'll ever create, without spending a penny more on marketing or promotions.

---

4. Source: Sun Tzu, "The Art of War", Dover edition, 2002, The Military Service Publishing Company, Harrisburg, Pennsylvania, ISBN 0-486-42557-6.

Action Steps

The best way to learn is to take the ball and run with it. At the end of each chapter, you'll find Action Steps that will guide you as you put what you've learned into practice.

1. Think of a current or past situation in which you or someone you work made the assumption that you didn't need to plan for some contingency because you probably wouldn't have competition. Now that you about the dangers of thinking "maybe they won't come", what would you do differently?

2. Take a situation, present or past, in which you've needed to get your people to willingly work overtime on a project. Can you think of any ways in which you could make it even more attractive to guard the "Great Wall of China"?

3. Visualize your company's infrastructure, both the physical plant and the people who work the front office. Now put yourself in the shoes of a customer walking in. What sort of impression do you get? How can you shore up inadequacies that you see in your infrastructure?

4. Think back to a time when you achieved a victory, didn't follow it up, and then things slipped through your fingers. What would you do differently now? Now think of a current victory you

17

are pursuing. What will you do after you get it to ensure a continuing success?

5. Do you know what information you need for the campaigns you're currently planning? If so, do you have all that information in hand? If not, what do you need to do to get it?

6. Think about conflicts that your company or team has right now. If you can't think of any, think of personal conflicts you have. Is there a temptation to buy peace? Now that you know the consequences, what can you do to dissuade your team members that this might not be the best course of action? If it's a personal conflict you have, think of ways you can stand up for what you believe and not give in to trying to make the other person like you.

Chapter 3

HOW TO GUARANTEE INCREDIBLE SUCCESS AND MAKE FAILURE NOT AN OPTION—LAYING PLANS

E ver had something fall apart because you just didn't know what your goals were? With the information I'm going to share with you in this chapter, that won't ever happen again! Read on, and learn how to plan a campaign, and what to stay away from…

No one plans to fail, they just fail to plan. Any military man or woman will tell you that proper planning is key. After all, surgical strikes don't just happen by themselves. The modern equivalent of Sun Tzu's military planning is the marketing campaign.

If you're tempted to skip this chapter because you think you're not in the marketing business, think again. No matter what business you think you're in, if you don't sell your product and services (or if your marketing group doesn't sell), your paychecks will soon come to a screeching, grinding halt.

And on a personal level, with job-hopping on the rise, you must always be prepared to sell yourself to a new company should you need to make a change.

The best marketing campaigns are thoughtfully planned and carefully designed so as to take maximum advantage of your product's strength and your competitors' weaknesses. To do this, your campaign should ideally:

- Be narrowly focused

- Center around one single concept or message

- Represent a single, unified effort

- Target a small niche

Smart people don't attack cities

In a perfect world, you wouldn't have to worry about competition. Sun Tzu recommends you attack while the enemy is still planning, which means either getting into a market first, or finding an overlooked market that your competitors just aren't tapping. This is the easiest way to succeed.

You think there aren't overlooked markets in our modern world? Here's a hint: look for the backlash against any current trend. Almost every major company in the US now uses automated voice-recognition software to handle your calls. Some people love VRUs, but there's a sizeable number of people who hate it. Think there's a market for a company that offers good old-fashioned live humans taking calls?

Second best, after finding an overlooked market, is to win over your competitor's suppliers or distributors. You've just breathed new life into your company and cut the legs out from underneath your enemy.

Third best is to go head-to-head against a competitor, with roughly the same time sequence. You launch something new, they launch something new, and may the better product win. You can also make their product obsolete by making a new and improved version of it. Then your job is to convince the consumer that the upgrade is worth it.

The very last thing you want to have to do is to launch a product or service that competes against an established product that's built up some good name recognition and brand loyalty. Sun Tzu refers to this as "attacking a city." This was what Coca-Cola did to themselves by bringing out New Coke and retiring the original—they attacked their very own city. How dumb was that?

OK, so you're probably wondering how an established product or service is like an ancient Chinese city. It's a metaphor. Ancient cities were walled to keep out attackers. The modern marketing equivalent of those walls is brand loyalty and familiarity. That's what you've got to overcome when you go up against an established product.

Why is it so tough? Because you've got to spend months developing a product that's not just as good, but better. Then you've got to design a campaign, which costs money to do, and implement it, which costs more. And even then you may not sway your target market.

If you don't get market share right away, you may resort to going negative by attacking the integrity of your competitor. This is nasty business and it usually backfires by making you look like third-rate, mud-slinging politico. As Sun Tzu says, "This attack is a disaster."[5]

21

Avoid competing against established products.

5. Source: Sun Tzu, "The Art of War", Dover edition, 2002, The Military Service Publishing Company, Harrisburg, Pennsylvania, ISBN 0-486-42557-6.

The Big 5 things you must know to run your next campaign

When you go to design a marketing campaign, or any other type of campaign to win anything, you must take into account five critical governing factors. I've listed the original Sun Tzu title first, then given the modern equivalent.

1. The Moral Law—Obedience and loyalty of the people carrying out the campaign. Will they do what you instruct them to do? Are they loyal, or will they leak costly information to the competition down at Happy Hour?

2. Heaven, also called "nature"—This refers to conditions that you cannot control. In Sun Tzu's time, it meant the weather, the darkness, the seasons, and the occasional flood or earthquake. For you, it means market conditions, the whims of the consumer, and world events (picture a Motel 6 fifty miles from New Orleans after Hurricane Katrina hit—they were full for a long, long time.)

3. Earth—These are conditions that you control. They include the timing of when to enter the market, who you hire, how you train them, and what market niche you select.

4. The Commander—This, of course, is your leader, or senior management. In Sun Tzu's day he stood for wisdom, sincerity, benevolence, courage, and strictness. Now he or she stands for savvy, integrity, giving to the United Way, being pro-active, and practicing the 7 Habits of Highly Effective People.

5. Method and Discipline—This is your organization and your process. Every marketing campaign is different, but

you still need a process for coming up with those clever little gems.

Getting the results you want instead of letting things happen

Begin with the end in mind. Too often, marketing campaigns start at the beginning. Visualize the end result and work backwards from there.

Realistically, even if you find an overlooked niche market, you won't be alone for long. You'll have company soon. Before you even launch your product, consider how you can inveigle your competitors into surrendering that market share to you. Indian businessman Harsh Mishra, of Bay Bridge Enterprises, LLC, got a contract from the U.S. government to haul off a fifty-year-old Navy submarine-rescue ship, the Sunbird. No one else wanted the Sunbird because it was old, it was dirty, and it smelled. It also had some interesting environmental hazards.

But Mishra accepted $85,900 from the U.S. government to haul it off because it contained $300,000 worth of salvageable steel, along with numerous engines, anchors and propellers, which were sold separately. As Mishra put it, staring down into the dank interior of the stinking wreck, *"Money doesn't always look pretty."*[6] Sun Tzu would have liked Mishra—he made money without having to compete for it.

If you are planning to enter a competitive marketplace, think of how you will win customers away from their current suppliers. What's your edge? What do you do, what do you

7. Source: *The Wall Street Journal*, January 10, 2006 edition, first column, page A1.

offer, or how do you deal with customers that they can't find anywhere else? Remember the car company, Saturn? They dealt with customers differently, and a certain segment of the market loved it.

You can win customers away, but your marketing campaign needs to be like a successful military battle: focused, short, concentrated, and swift.

One of the worst mistakes you can make is to stop selling when you hit your target. This goes back to "always follow up a victory." What do you think happened to the ancient Chinese warriors when they conquered a territory and stopped there? Before too long, those pesky Tatars or someone similar would come along to challenge ownership.

Never stop selling. Never take the customer for granted. This is why you get Christmas cards and "thank-you" gifts from companies you've done business with for years. It's why "Customer Appreciation" days exist.

Making numbers work for you in planning

Sun Tzu gave some detailed numerical formulas for planning. In the modern world, they go like this:

- If you have distribution that's ten times that of your next competitor, you *will* kick butt in the market.

- If you have distribution that's five times greater, launch your product aggressively.

- If you have distribution that's twice as good, your best bet is to segment the market, or divide it.

- If you have distribution is equal to your competitors, pick the low-hanging fruit. Target your marketing to the best prospects.

- If you have distribution that's weaker, don't position your products where the competition is strong.

- If you have distribution that's much weaker, you need to find your own little niche...and while you're at it, take care of that lame distribution system.

Little companies are best off in niche markets, not broad ones. Big companies can compete in the big markets, but may have trouble satisfying niche markets in which customer expectations are high.

Sales people can sometimes create new problems. You probably knew that, but maybe you don't know why. Sun Tzu had a theory about that. His philosophy applied to politicians and the army, but it's quite apropos to sales persons and your organization. Sales staff can cause problems in three main ways.

If your sales reps don't know who the best prospects are, they'll waste time going after everyone. Teach them how to pre-qualify the best prospects. Another mistake occurs when sales reps don't realize they're in a no-win market and they waste time trying to sell anyway, ignoring their current customers.

Yet a third mistake—and this is the biggie—happens when sales reps just plain don't understand marketing and the try to make it up as they go along. This is particularly bad for morale, since it indicates a lack of trust in the organization. Educate them that they don't make marketing strategy, just carry it out.

25

The 7 key things to know about your organization

When you're sizing up your competition, you're looking for strengths and weaknesses relative to your own. Here are seven key questions that you should ask.

1. Who has the most loyal people?

2. Who has the most competent managers?

3. Who's got the market conditions in his favor?

4. Who's got the best-run organization?

5. Who's got the best all-around people?

6. Who's got the most highly trained people?

7. Which organization has the most discipline?

When you plan, you have to know when you should enter a market and when you should stay out of it. If your largest competitor has just done a big, splashy launch of a product that creates real excitement, give it time to die down.

You must also choose an appropriate market size and focus on it, otherwise you waste money. If your product is satellite dish TV, why market it to everyone with a TV, including city people who have cable? Why not stick to rural markets, where satellite dish is the only way they can get TV?

Every time you see what appears to be a problem (or *issue*, for fans of political correctness), look past it to see the underlying opportunity. Lead the market, don't follow it. Be Coke, not Pepsi. Win the trust of your sales people by giving them a product that they can wholeheartedly endorse and they'll sell the living daylights out of it for you.

Put yourself in the driver's seat of the market

Sun Tzu said, "Know yourself and know your enemy."7 To which Clint Eastwood would add, "A man's got to know his limitations." When you design a marketing campaign, know your own strengths and weaknesses, and know your target market. If you do, you can win significant market share. If you don't, you'll waste resources. It's as simple as that.

Warfare is based on deception. In marketing, we practice deception. Not with respect to the customer—there are laws against false advertising—but with respect to our competitors. We want to give those guys and gals a false appearance.

When you're in a position to sell, you want the competition to think you're not, or that you're not really trying. When you're mounting a campaign, you need to look like you're idle. When you're close, you want to seem far away. When you're far away from a launch, you want them to think you're close.

Don't be afraid to bait the competition and drop false rumors in bars and conferences. Act like you're disorganized, like you don't have your act together…then crush them.

To that end, you might want to reassess what you wear to trade shows. If you're not working the company booth, don't wear the company shirt as you wander the aisles talking to people. And if you can use another credential on your name tag, go for it. Then start asking questions. It's called being a good spy, and Chinese warfare was full of them.

If your competition is:

- Secure—Be prepared.

- Superior—Run.

27

- Has a temper—Provoke him or her.

- Inactive—Run him or her ragged, giving no chance to rest.

Get my drift? Always, and I do mean always, do the unexpected. Don't be predictable. If you start following a pattern, abruptly change it just when they seem to be catching on.

Women do this all the time and men don't realize it. Men know strength. Men are strong. Men know how to handle strength. So the worst thing a woman can do is come on too strong. If she does, the man will just stiff-arm her. He knows how to counter strength. Ah, but when she acts disinterested and isn't there…the man doesn't know what to do, so he runs after her. Be like the smart women.

Wow, that's a lot of great stuff you've absorbed on planning, isn't it? But a plan is nothing without action. In the next chapter, I'll show you how to hit the ground running by putting your plan into action so that you bring in the bucks.

28

Action Steps

1. Think of five different ways in which you've marketed yourself in the last year. Now think ahead to the coming year. What ways do you foresee marketing yourself?

2. Consider your current marketing campaign, along with any other that you have planned. Are you trying to attack a city (i.e., an established product or service?)

3. What one concrete step can you take this week to improve your marketing with respect to each of the following: loyalty and obedience, conditions you can't control, conditions you can control, leadership, and your organization? Now take them.

4. Touch base with your sales reps and make sure they know who their target customers are, how to pre-qualify them, and that they fully understand their role with respect to marketing.

5. Identify the competitor that poses the biggest current threat, and answer the 7 key questions about your organization versus theirs. After you do this, you may wish to reassess your marketing strategy.

6. List three problems your marketing has. Now, brainstorm to discover the underlying opportunity.

7. List three ways that you have deceived your competitors in the past. List three ways that you can deceive them in the future, or, even better, in your current marketing campaign.

29

ORIGINAL TEXT: Laying Plans

1. *Sun Tzu said: The art of war is of vital importance to the State.*

2. *It is a matter of life and death, a road either to safety or to ruin. Hence it is a subject of inquiry which can on no account be neglected.*

3. *The art of war, then, is governed by five constant factors, to be taken into account in one's deliberations, when seeking to determine the conditions obtaining in the field.*

4. *These are: (1) The Moral Law; (2) Heaven; (3) Earth; (4) The Commander; (5) Method and discipline.*

5.,6. *The Moral Law causes the people to be in complete accord with their ruler, so that they will follow him regardless of their lives, undismayed by any danger.*

7. *Heaven signifies night and day, cold and heat, times and seasons.*

8. *Earth comprises distances, great and small; danger and security; open ground and narrow passes; the chances of life and death.*

9. *The Commander stands for the virtues of wisdom, sincerely, benevolence, courage and strictness.*

10. *By method and discipline are to be understood the marshaling of the army in its proper subdivisions, the graduations of rank among the officers, the*

maintenance of roads by which supplies may reach the army, and the control of military expenditure.

11. *These five heads should be familiar to every general: he who knows them will be victorious; he who knows them not will fail.*

12. *Therefore, in your deliberations, when seeking to determine the military conditions, let them be made the basis of a comparison, in this wise:—*

13. (1) *Which of the two sovereigns is imbued with the Moral law?*

    (2) *Which of the two generals has most ability?*

    (3) *With whom lie the advantages derived from Heaven and Earth?*

    (4) *On which side is discipline most rigorously enforced?*

    (5) *Which army is stronger?*

    (6) *On which side are officers and men more highly trained?*

    (7) *In which army is there the greater constancy both in reward and punishment?*

14. *By means of these seven considerations I can forecast victory or defeat.*

15. *The general that hearkens to my counsel and acts upon it, will conquer: let such a one be retained in command! The general that hearkens not to my*

counsel nor acts upon it, will suffer defeat:—let such a one be dismissed!

16. While heading the profit of my counsel, avail yourself also of any helpful circumstances over and beyond the ordinary rules.

17. According as circumstances are favorable, one should modify one's plans.

18. All warfare is based on deception.

19. Hence, when able to attack, we must seem unable; when using our forces, we must seem inactive; when we are near, we must make the enemy believe we are far away; when far away, we must make him believe we are near.

20. Hold out baits to entice the enemy. Feign disorder, and crush him.

21. If he is secure at all points, be prepared for him. If he is in superior strength, evade him.

22. If your opponent is of choleric temper, seek to irritate him. Pretend to be weak, that he may grow arrogant.

23. If he is taking his ease, give him no rest. If his forces are united, separate them.

24. Attack him where he is unprepared, appear where you are not expected.

25. These military devices, leading to victory, must not be divulged beforehand.

26. *Now the general who wins a battle makes many calculations in his temple ere the battle is fought. The general who loses a battle makes but few calculations beforehand. Thus do many calculations lead to victory, and few calculations to defeat: how much more no calculation at all! It is by attention to this point that I can foresee who is likely to win or lose.*

33

Chapter 4

GENERATE INCREDIBLE PROFITS BY RUNNING AN EFFECTIVE CAMPAIGN— WAGING WAR

Planning's great, but it doesn't put product out into the hands of customers and—most importantly—get them to fork over their hard-earned money. How do you make the leap from the well-laid plans of mice and men to waging war for customer dollars? Stick with me and I'll tell you in this chapter.

After the U.S. went to war in Iraq in 2003, Secretary of Defense Donald Rumsfeld was asked by a member of the press why the military didn't have enough armor plating to protect it's Humvees. Rumsfeld replies, "You have to go to war with the Army you have, not the Army you want."

A very appropriate follow-up question would have been, "Why not make sure you have the army you want before you launch into a war?"

The must-have resources

You don't ever want to be in Secretary Rumsfeld's position, fielding tough questions about why you launched a major marketing campaign without adequate commitment from your personnel, an adequate budget, or adequate creativity.

Once you determine your market strategy, go through it and list the resources that you will need to carry it out. Think in terms of personnel, money, ad space, and any venues you may need to book.

Actually, the term "adequate" is probably not, well…*adequate*. There's an old military saying that "No battle plan survives contact with the enemy." What this means is that it's one thing to plan your campaign from the cozy confines of a conference room, when you're not under any kind of intense pressure. It's quite another thing to try to stick to your plan when, despite your best intelligence, your closest competitor launches a better product the day after you launched your latest effort.

Therefore, it's best to go into a campaign with more resources than you think you'll need. Know what the number one reason is that start-ups fail? "We ran out of money."[8] And usually, that statement is followed by "We could have made money if we hadn't run out of capital." Airline start-ups are notorious for this, since it takes an enormous amount of capital to purchase planes, rent space at an airport, set up terminals, and put the necessary people in place to staff the first flight.

Undercapitalization is an easy mistake to make. If you can't line up sufficient cash on hand, supplement it with business lines of credit, or make an arrangement in advance with your suppliers.

Why does running out of money kill start-ups? Because they haven't yet built their customer base. They may also lack the expertise necessary to pull off victory, and their staff may be less than fully seasoned.

---

8. Source: Sun Tzu, "The Art of War", Dover edition, 2002, The Military Service Publishing Company, Harrisburg, Pennsylvania, ISBN 0-486-42557-6.

How much money to allocate? That's the tricky part. It's prudent to set a limit, so that at some point you cut your losses. On the other hand, if you are absolutely, 100% certain you can win, then do what you need to do.

To determine if your budget is adequate, you will need some idea of how long you expect this campaign to last, which brings us to our next topic...

What's the shelf life of your campaign?

Sun Tzu said, *"When you engage in actual fighting, if victory is long in coming, then men's weapons will grow dull and their ardor will be damped."*

Too much of anything, even if it's a wonderful thing, is not good. Long, protracted marketing campaigns are something you want to avoid if at all possible because:

- Your people will become mentally fatigued and lose their edge.

- Your target market will get tired of your ads and tune them out.

Campaigns should have a definite start and end date. No matter how skilled your marketing staff is, they won't be able to sustain a continuous of high excitement. It is very easy to pour money and energy into a campaign, but not so easy to disengage. Learn the fine art of disengagement.

Turning time into money

On the highways and in the underground world of drugs, speed kills. But in business, it's a must-have. Speed is the efficient

37

use of time. Napoleon knew this, and he knew that the military standard was to have troops march at 70 paces per minute. So Mr. Original-Go-Getter Bonaparte had his troops march at 120 paces per minute. Result? His guys got there faster, and won the territory.[9]

There is an optimum speed, and it's the one at which you're not making mistakes but you're not slow, either. One of the big developments of the last few decades was the time-to-market cycle. When you shorten the cycle of identifying a niche to putting product on the shelves, you gain a competitive advantage.

Technology is changing so fast that some say we are approaching what the science-fiction people call a "singularity"—a point at which everything is happening at once. I don't know about that, but I do know that when you're Dell Computer, you'd better get your new PC on the market pronto before it becomes outdated by the latest Gateway Computer release.

Time can be your friend. When you're the first one in a new market, consumers have no other option. Of course, you don't want dissatisfied customers, so you need to make sure that whatever you put on the market is as good as you can make it.

You also need to make sure you have the support system in place so that when the inevitable phone calls and e-mails drift in, asking about your product or raising some sort of issue about a purchase, you can be there for your customers.

The advice I've given you above sounds simple, but the business graveyard is littered with the bones of companies who underestimated what it takes to support a product.

---

9. Source: Sun Tzu, "The Art of War", Dover edition, 2002, The Military Service Publishing Company, Harrisburg, Pennsylvania, ISBN 0-486-42557-6.

Remember that TV commercial in which the roomful of techies rejoices as the internet counter that takes orders for their product flips from "0" to "1"? Remember how happy they were? And do you remember how their joyful smiles froze, then turned to blind panic when the counter hit 10,000 right before their eyes? They had that reaction because they had no infrastructure to support 10,000 sales.

Make your competitors feed you

Sun Tsu said, *"Bring war material with you from home, but forage on the enemy."* In the 21st century, this means leveraging your competitors, their distribution systems, and the media in your marketing efforts.

Why devote time and resources to carving out your own distribution system from scratch when you can use one of your competitor's distribution systems?

Small, local newspapers do this all the time, with great success. You probably have one of those rags where you live…little weekly newspaper or magazine that you pick up for free at the grocery store or gym. They're supported by advertising, and they usually run on a shoestring. So how can they afford a printing press plant?

They can't, and they don't. Every city of any size has at least one daily newspaper, complete with printing presses. The small weeklies go to them, and for a fee, do a secondary run that prints their rag after the daily has been run for the day.

Maybe you can't afford the distribution chain of a big player, but you can probably catch a ride on their train. One caution, though: don't waste your time with the really big outfits like Wal-Mart, Home Depot, or Dell Computer. They have their own proprietary distribution networks that handle their stuff and no one else's. They're too big to need to share.

Another way in which you can forage off of your competitors is simply by overflow. Pay attention to the marketplace…is your competitor's product backordered? Have they been forced to do a recall? When something like that happens, you need to be in a position to jump right in with both feet.

Everyone wins where there's victory

Sun Tsu speaks of rousing your men to anger during a campaign. Obviously, true anger is more suited to war, but what you can take from this is that you must have your people's buy-in prior to launching a campaign. You must always make sure that your people understand that they have a personal stake in victory.

This is why it is better to put sales staff on commission rather than paying them a salary or an hourly rate. The more a sales person sells, and the bigger the sale, the more he or she makes.

While you wouldn't want to put your entire staff on commission, you do want to make it abundantly clear that you will reward victories and outstanding personal performances with a cash bonus. When your people know there's money for them at stake, they will work harder and longer.

And do make it a cash bonus—no trophies, plaques, or golf shirts please. Many companies have conducted study after study which has consistently shown that employees greatly prefer cash over anything else. Trinkets just don't cut it.

If your campaign is long, think of ways in which you can give interim rewards for milestones achieved. You want to make that reward cycle as short as possible, and give out the bonuses immediately following the victory. Make sure you do it in front of an audience, too. As the old saying goes, "Praise publicly, reprimand privately."

When a competitor does a lay-off, start the rumor mill buzzing that you might be in the market for a few people. Sun Tsu recommends, "...*using the conquered foe to augment one's own strength.*" There is a wealth of information you can gain from someone who was recently laid-off from a competitor. Sure, they probably signed a non-disclosure agreement. But things will invariably slip. There's also the benefit of gaining an employee who already knows the business you're in.

Have you learned a lot about how to run a campaign? It's a lot to take in, I know, but right now light bulbs should be going off in your head concerning your marketing campaigns. Exciting, huh? Well, you haven't seen anything yet—in the next chapter I'm going to teach you some of the sneakiest strategy you've ever seen. Hang in there, and I'll show you how to win without even fighting, among other things!

41

Action Steps:

1. List the resources that you will need for a campaign you're currently planning, or one that you envision in the future. Be sure to include people, materials, budget, air time, rented venue space, and overhead.

2. Think about your last campaign. How long did it last? In retrospect, was it too long? Now think about a campaign you're planning. Do you think it's too long or too short?

3. List ten ways in which you, your employees, or your marketing group has wasted time in the past. Now, for each, list a pro-active way in which you can minimize that time-waster in the future.

4. Make a spreadsheet of employees who came from other companies, and list the companies. When a competitor does a lay-off, approach your employees who used to work at that company and ask for leads on recently-laid off personnel.

5. List five ways in which you can make a marketing victory benefit everyone in your organization. Make sure you include project milestones and cash.

ORIGINAL TEXT: Waging War

1. Sun Tzu said: "In the operations of war, where there are in the field a thousand swift chariots, as many heavy chariots, and a hundred thousand mail-clad soldiers, with provisions enough to carry them a thousand li, the expenditure at home and at the front, including entertainment of guests, small items such as glue and paint, and sums spent on chariots and armor, will reach the total of a thousand ounces of silver per day. Such is the cost of raising an army of 100,000 men.

2. When you engage in actual fighting, if victory is long in coming, then men's weapons will grow dull and their ardor will be damped. If you lay siege to a town, you will exhaust your strength.

3. Again, if the campaign is protracted, the resources of the State will not be equal to the strain.

4. Now, when your weapons are dulled, your ardor damped, your strength exhausted and your treasure spent, other chieftains will spring up to take advantage of your extremity. Then no man, however wise, will be able to avert the consequences that must ensue.

5. Thus, though we have heard of stupid haste in war, cleverness has never been seen associated with long delays.

6. There is no instance of a country having benefited from prolonged warfare.

7. It is only one who is thoroughly acquainted with the evils of war that can thoroughly understand the profitable way of carrying it on.

8. The skillful soldier does not raise a second levy, neither are his supply-wagons loaded more than twice.

9. Bring war material with you from home, but forage on the enemy. Thus the army will have food enough for its needs.

10. Poverty of the State exchequer causes an army to be maintained by contributions from a distance. Contributing to maintain an army at a distance causes the people to be impoverished.

11. On the other hand, the proximity of an army causes prices to go up; and high prices cause the people's substance to be drained away.

12. When their substance is drained away, the peasantry will be afflicted by heavy exactions.

13,14. With this loss of substance and exhaustion of strength, the homes of the people will be stripped bare, and three-tenths of their income will be dissipated; while government expenses for broken chariots, worn-out horses, breast-plates and helmets, bows and arrows, spears and shields, protective mantles, draught-oxen and heavy wagons, will amount to four-tenths of its total revenue.

44

15. *Hence a wise general makes a point of foraging on the enemy. One cartload of the enemy's provisions is equivalent to twenty of one's own, and likewise a single picul of his provender is equivalent to twenty from one's own store.*

16. *Now in order to kill the enemy, our men must be roused to anger; that there may be advantage from defeating the enemy, they must have their rewards.*

17. *Therefore in chariot fighting, when ten or more chariots have been taken, those should be rewarded who took the first. Our own flags should be substituted for those of the enemy, and the chariots mingled and used in conjunction with ours. The captured soldiers should be kindly treated and kept.*

45

18. *This is called, using the conquered foe to augment one's own strength.*

19. *In war, then, let your great object be victory, not lengthy campaigns.*

20. *Thus it may be known that the leader of armies is the arbiter of the people's fate, the man on whom it depends whether the nation shall be in peace or in peril.*

Chapter 5

SETTING STRATEGY THAT'S SNEAKY AS HELL

E ver wanted to grab market share without having to campaign long and hard for it? Maybe you don't relish a protracted battle that drains your marketing budget? Good news—you don't have to go there! In this chapter, I'm going to share some sneaky strategy with you, also known as "the lazy man's marketing."

Why bother with something as esoteric-sounding as strategy? Why not just get out there and sell? Because you'll get your ass handed to you, that's why. Prussian military theorist General Carl von Clausewitz (1780-1831) explained that strategy is vital because it tells you *where* to hit *when*, and with *how much force*.[10]

Wouldn't that be great if you could know exactly where to put your advertising, along with what time slot, and how much to saturate the market? Well, you can…it just takes a little homework in advance. It starts by identifying who your customer is, and they may not be who you think they are. Take Duct-tape, for instance.

Duct-tape was originally a very specific product. It was designed to tape up ventilation and air-conditioning ducts in

---

10. Source: "On War", by General Carl von Clausewitz, N. Trübner, London, 1873.

homes and businesses, hence the name (commonly misspelled as "duck tape.") But then HVAC repair people found themselves using the tough tape for all sorts of other uses. They started loaning it out to friends and neighbors, and it never came back.

Thus, an all-purpose legend was born. Now it's used for everything from repairing junker cars to protecting band-aided areas on adventure racers' feet to do-it-yourself hair removal. There are even two books listed on amazon.com that detail all the ways in which you can use duct tape. The point is, the makers of duct tape assumed a much narrower customer base than they actually had.

Once you know your customer, analyze his needs and wants. What need does he have that isn't being filled? Don't hesitate to ask. One way of increasing your business, by the way, is to ask current customers what else they need—in addition to your product—to complete whatever it is they're doing.

Let me stimulate your brain with a few examples. There are whole new companies that have sprung up in the last few decades because:

- People wanted to carry a cup of coffee in the car without it spilling—Travel and commuter mugs, complete with snap-on lids and a lever to turn to drink.

- People wanted an inexpensive way to show off their status and they were willing to shift from seeing coffee as a commodity to a branded product—Starbucks.

- People needed a way to add air to their vehicle tires without driving on low tires to a service station or buying a costly air compressor—Fix-A-Flat cans that screw onto the valve and inflate the tire, approximately $7 each.

When you mount a campaign to increase market share, you are out to steal it from your competitors. In doing that, you want that market share intact. Sun Tzu said: *"...the best thing of all is to take the enemy's country whole and intact; to shatter and destroy it is not so good."* This is why most marketing campaigns carefully avoid going negative. You don't want to slam the competition or their products too much, because some of that will rub off on the entire industry.

Free money is great—get it without fighting

As I said earlier, the best use of resources is not to use them at all, or as little as possible, to get what you want. When Starbucks started aggressively expanding their chain of coffeehouses, they had virtually no competition other than small mom-and-pop operations. No one else was growing a regional or national chain, since coffee was still largely viewed as a commodity and bought on the basis of price.

You don't have to forge a whole new market like Starbucks did. Sun Tzu advises generals to place their strength where the enemy is weak, and the Holiday Inn motel chain did exactly that when they decide to put their motels along interstate highways and other major roadways on the edges of cities and towns.

Holiday Inn did this for two reasons. The primary one was that they didn't have to directly compete against established hotel chains like Hilton and Sheraton which were located in the heart of cities. A secondary reason was that land prices and taxes were lower on the outskirts, which gave Holiday Inn less overhead, allowing them to offer lower prices.

Once you're either first in a new market (that perhaps you've created), or first in an area where your competitors aren't, you need to start working on building customer loyalty. You won't be alone for long, so take advantage of the time you have as the only one to build strong customer loyalty so that when the competition arrives, you won't lose too many customers. Never let yourself get lulled into thinking that you've got it good since you're the only player in the market, because that *will not last.*

Be strong where they're weak

Sun Tsu teaches to be where the enemy is not, and to show strength where he is weak. That's a great strategy, but if you get into a market first, don't expect the enemy to not be there forever. Likewise, if you pour resources into a huge marketing campaign in a market where the competition has only a weak presence ("being strong where he is weak"), don't expect that to last, either. Use the time you have effectively to build your base of loyal customers as fast as possible, because competition *will come.*

In 1980, IBM decided that desktop personal computers were going to be the new thing, so they set out to build the hardware for them. There was just one problem—they didn't have an operating system to run those computers. So they went to one of their favorite non-IBM go-to guys, Bill Gates.

Gates referred them to Digital Research, who made CP/M, which was just about the only game in town back then for operating systems. But IBM and the founder of Digital Research were unable to come to terms immediately, and IBM needed an operating system ASAP. So they went back to their go-to guy.

DAN LOK & SUN TSU

Sensing the opportunity to be strong where his competition was weak, Gates told IBM he would take care of it himself. Then he bought a CP/M clone called QDOS ("Quick and Dirty Operating System") from Tim Paterson of Seattle Computer Products for $56,000 and renamed it PC-DOS. He licensed it to IBM, and later renamed it MS-DOS (Microsoft Disk Operating System.)

The rest, as they say, is history. Gates succeeded because he saw a weakness in the negotiations between IBM and the founder of Digital Research. Microsoft has since made a fortune in being strong where others are weak.

Fertile ground for weaknesses in the competition include underserved markets. Prior to the 1990's, if you had bad credit, you just plain couldn't get a credit card due to laws regulating interest rates. In other words, lenders couldn't charge high enough interest rates to make a pool of bad risks worthwhile.

Enter secured credit cards. They were developed and marketed when an enterprising lender figured out that there was a large market that:

1. Needed a credit card to book airline flights, buy gas, order from catalogues, and other things.

2. Had bad credit.

3. Wanted a second chance to repair their credit.

Thus was born the secured credit card. It works like this: you deposit $500 with the company, and they issue you a card with a $500 limit. It's really no different than a checking account, except that it is a bona fide credit card and thus all activity is reported to the big three credit reporting companies: Trans-Union, Equifax, and Experian. There is very little risk to

51

the credit card company, and the process allows the consumer to rebuild their credit by paying on time. It's a win-win.

The first credit card company to offer the secured credit card won market share because they were bold enough to enter a market where others had feared to tread.

Ways in which you can exploit competitor weaknesses include:

- Finding fault in your competitors' products and making sure your product addresses those faults—think of the dishwasher detergent commercials in which "leading brands" leave spots on glasses, but the one being advertised doesn't.

- Going into an underserved market and claiming it.

- Capitalizing on a misstep by a competitor—when they have a big, public lawsuit or a recall, that's the time to lay it on thick and stress the wonderful qualities of your product.

Connect your disconnects

Sun Tsu warns against rulers bringing misfortune upon their army by giving orders that can't be obeyed (hobbling the army), trying to run an army like a kingdom, or interfering with the direction of fighting.

What's all that mean? Well, the part about giving orders that can't be obeyed implies that the ruler—that's you, by the way—is out of touch with his organizational reality. If your marketing organization doesn't have the key players, the budget, or the collateral available for a campaign, no amount of high-dollar motivational speakers is going to get them moving.

Another way to hobble your army with an order that can't be obeyed is to send them against the equivalent of a walled city. If you're a start-up computer hardware company, you don't go head-to-head with IBM. Software? Don't try to compete against Microsoft in their core products. Instead, search for something IBM or Microsoft are overlooking, some market that's not worth their time because there's only, oh, ten million bucks or so in profit to be had.

Why not try to run an army like a kingdom? It's the classic difference between a wartime general and a peacetime king. They require different animals. Your marketing people are your army—they're out there waging a guerilla war for market share. The rest of your organization isn't fighting a war. They don't need a general, they need a king or a president. Kings and presidents don't usually have to make quick decisions—they have the luxury of being able to sit back, discuss, debate, and deliberate.

53

The worst way to shoot yourself in the foot is by interfering with the direction of fighting. Nowadays we call that "micromanaging." It's bad for several reasons:

1. It wastes your time. You hire competent managers—let them do their jobs.

2. It sends a dangerous message that you don't trust your people to make decisions. As time goes on, they will internalize that and thus, become unable to make decisions.

3. It's just plain bad for your stress level. Expect an ulcer or heart attack if you micromanage.

4. You lose your best people because they'll go work for a company that cares about empowering them.

They had a good system in the Prussian army, back before Prussia was taken over by Germany. In the late nineteenth century, the Prussians drew a clear distinction between an *order* and an *instruction*. *Instructions* were what the general wanted to happen, and it was left to the field commander to carry it out when it was feasible to do so. *Orders*, however, had to be obeyed literally and instantly, and could only be given by an officer who was right there in the trenches with the troops and who knew what was really going on.

Telling your marketing crew to get your new product placed at the ends of aisles in stores is an instruction. The crew will do the best they can, but if a particular store has no room right then, or if another product is in that spot right now, they'll have to figure out something else.

Telling your marketing crew not to price the product below $9.95 after you have reviewed a thorough market analysis is an order.

Knowing what the hell you're doing

OK, I know the title above might sound a bit extreme, but you'd be surprised. During the dot-com boom of the late 90's, fledgling start-ups flush with venture capital were frequently captained by twenty-somethings who had no clue what a realistic business environment looked like, nor how to conduct themselves within one.

Sun Tsu said, in so many words:

- Know when to fight and when not to fight.

- Know how to leverage a great organization as well as a crappy one.

- The organization with the best teamwork wins.

- Be prepared and ready to move and you'll beat competitors who aren't.

- Empower your marketing managers and don't get in their way.

There are times to market, and times to not market (right when a superior competitor is doing a big, splashy launch.) It's great to be able to run a terrific organization, but a true leader should be able to lead a so-so organization—it's all about knowing your strengths and weaknesses. Turn-around artists like Jack Welch, former CEO of General Electric, and "Chainsaw" Al Dunlap of Sunbeam are prime examples of leaders who took the reins of struggling organizations and turned them around.

As far as teamwork, look no further than Avis Rent-a-Car. Back in the sixties, they lagged behind Hertz by quite a bit. They pulled their marketing together and managed to use Hertz' size and success against them (turning a strength into a weakness, which Sun Tsu would have loved) with a campaign slogan, "We Try Harder." Follow up commercials showed Hertz reps acting like fat cats who didn't have to try hard, while Avis portrayed themselves as willing to go many extra miles for the customer. It worked.

The dot-com bust of 2000 may have been horrible for many, but for a savvy few it represented opportunity. You see, they were prepared and ready to move when things started to go south. Who did well in the aftermath of the dog-com bust? Well, used office furniture brokers, for one. Also fix-and-flip real estate investors, who were able to buy up foreclosed homes cheap and resell them.

55

Remember this: every change represents opportunity. Even in the midst of the Great Depression, or the dot-com bust of 2000, there were those who were prepared, so they saw the opportunities, and they took action.

The last bit about not getting in your managers' way should be obvious, but it's not. Let your people work for you—that's what you pay them for.

There's been a whole lot to take in during this chapter, but by now you know how to be sneaky as hell, get free money by being strong where your competitors are weak, connect disconnects, and make sure your people are up to the task. How about implementing all that? Hang on, because in the next chapter I'll get down and dirty about tactics and show you how you just plain can't lose!

56

Action Steps:

1. Think of five current markets in which you can win without fighting. In particular, look for unserved or underserved markets. Now think about markets that no one's even thought of. Remember the Pet Rock?

2. Write down the names of your top three competitors. List their strong points, or markets in which they are strong. Now list markets where they could be, but are not. Point your marketing efforts in those directions.

3. Think of a time when you gave an order and your organization was unable to carry it out. Consider orders you may be planning to give in the future. Now, assess your organization to see what they can and can't do, realistically.

4. Look for disconnects within your organization. Here's a simple test: do the people in one department know the names of the people in other departments? Make sure everyone's on the same page and that communication is facilitated.

5. Here's a difficult one: assess your key players. Do they know what they're doing, or have they been promoted in line with the Peter Principle? That is, to their level of incompetence? (There was once technical manager who was demoted when it was discovered he had no idea what his labor rate was...or even what a labor rate was.)

57

ORIGINAL TEXT: Attack by Stratagem

1. *Sun Tzu said: In the practical art of war, the best thing of all is to take the enemy's country whole and intact; to shatter and destroy it is not so good. So, too, it is better to recapture an army entire than to destroy it, to capture a regiment, a detachment or a company entire than to destroy them.*

2. *Hence to fight and conquer in all your battles is not supreme excellence; supreme excellence consists in breaking the enemy's resistance without fighting.*

3. *Thus the highest form of generalship is to balk the enemy's plans; the next best is to prevent the junction of the enemy's forces; the next in order is to attack the enemy's army in the field; and the worst policy of all is to besiege walled cities.*

4. *The rule is, not to besiege walled cities if it can possibly be avoided. The preparation of mantlets, movable shelters, and various implements of war, will take up three whole months; and the piling up of mounds over against the walls will take three months more.*

5. *The general, unable to control his irritation, will launch his men to the assault like swarming ants, with the result that one-third of his men are slain, while the town still remains untaken. Such are the disastrous effects of a siege.*

6. *Therefore the skillful leader subdues the enemy's troops without any fighting; he captures their cities*

without laying siege to them; he overthrows their kingdom without lengthy operations in the field.

7. *With his forces intact he will dispute the mastery of the Empire, and thus, without losing a man, his triumph will be complete. This is the method of attacking by stratagem.*

8. *It is the rule in war, if our forces are ten to the enemy's one, to surround him; if five to one, to attack him; if twice as numerous, to divide our army into two.*

9. *If equally matched, we can offer battle; if slightly inferior in numbers, we can avoid the enemy; if quite unequal in every way, we can flee from him.*

10. *Hence, though an obstinate fight may be made by a small force, in the end it must be captured by the larger force.*

11. *Now the general is the bulwark of the State; if the bulwark is complete at all points; the State will be strong; if the bulwark is defective, the State will be weak.*

12. *There are three ways in which a ruler can bring misfortune upon his army:—*

13. *(1) By commanding the army to advance or to retreat, being ignorant of the fact that it cannot obey. This is called hobbling the army.*

14. *(2) By attempting to govern an army in the same way as he administers a kingdom, being ignorant of the conditions which obtain in an army. This causes restlessness in the soldier's minds.*

15. (3) By employing the officers of his army without discrimination, through ignorance of the military principle of adaptation to circumstances. This shakes the confidence of the soldiers.

16. But when the army is restless and distrustful, trouble is sure to come from the other feudal princes. This is simply bringing anarchy into the army, and flinging victory away.

17. Thus we may know that there are five essentials for victory:

    (1) He will win who knows when to fight and when not to fight.

    (2) He will win who knows how to handle both superior and inferior forces.

    (3) He will win whose army is animated by the same spirit throughout all its ranks.

    (4) He will win who, prepared himself, waits to take the enemy unprepared.

    (5) He will win who has military capacity and is not interfered with by the sovereign.

18. Hence the saying: If you know the enemy and know yourself, you need not fear the result of a hundred battles. If you know yourself but not the enemy, for every victory gained you will also suffer a defeat. If you know neither the enemy nor yourself, you will succumb in every battle.

Chapter 6

BECOME THE BIGGEST PLAYER IN YOUR MARKET WITH SUPERIOR POSITIONING— TACTICAL DISPOSITIONS

S trategy is great…but how to you carry it out? Well, that's what tactics are for, and in this chapter you'll learn how to become a terrific tactician who can carry out magnificent marketing campaigns. Read on, and learn…

61

You win by not losing…seriously!

What's a surefire way to win? Don't lose. Sound silly? Not to Sun Tsu it didn't…and not to top generals throughout history, along with modern executives like yourself who are clued in. Sun Tsu said, "The good fighter is able to secure himself against defeat, but cannot make certain of defeating the enemy." So what he's really talking about is taking steps to make sure—as much as possible—that you simply cannot lose.

Football teams know about this; it's called defense. One type of winning football team is the type that has an incredible offense and can score touchdown after touchdown. Another type may not have such a great offense, but they play great defense and prevent points from being scored *against them*. And then, at the highest levels, there are the teams that can do both…like the 2005 and 2006 University of Texas Longhorns, who won the Rose Bowl two years in a row and captured the National Championship in the latter bowl.

You want to be like the Longhorns, so it's worth your time to do some brainstorming on ways in which your marketing campaign can lose. How can you fail? How can things fall apart? Where could the ball be dropped? Who are your key players and what happens if they suddenly quit or get sick?

Once you've got those bug-a-boos on paper, start making back-up plans. A sample of potential problems and their solutions might look like this:

- Shipment X fails to arrive on time—Build in a few days buffer and if it hasn't arrived two days before we need it, we go get it or we buy from an alternate supplier that we've line up.

- John Doe, who handles all our customer accounts for this niche, quits or is incapacitated—we train another marketing person, Suzie Q, in what John does so that she can step in if necessary.

- A State of the Union address pre-empts our primo TV commercial spot—negotiate with the network to give us extra spots in the same time slot the next day.

Trying not to lose comes into play when you just can't find that hot new niche you'd like to locate and dominate. Sometimes it just won't show itself—that's life. When that happens, you can "not lose" by pulling in the reins and focusing on your existing customers. You probably already know it's much easier to get existing or former customers to buy from you than to go out and get new ones.

So why not start asking your customers what else they'd like to see you carry, or what else they need for whatever they're buying from you? You'd be surprised! Then, expand your product line. You won't lose. And eventually, you'll find that new niche.

This advice also holds true when you simply don't have the budget for a new marketing campaign to capture a new market. At that point, you need to hold onto what you've got. When you hit the point at which your income exceeds outgo, then you can start planning an expansion.

When you expand, Sun Tsu says, "You must defend yourself well." Don't neglect existing products or your competition will see weakness there. Conserve resources until you can identify a new niche and you've got the resources to be all over it.

Finesse your selling with creativity

63

One of the worst ways to lose is because of a lack of creativity. And believe me, it happens. One of the most common ways it happens is when you see a niche, and you know that those customers need and want what you can provide, but you just don't know how to brand and market your product in a way that they will accept.

Or perhaps you've branded your product and marketed it, and it's not the huge, smashing success that you know it should be. What do you do? You rebrand it. There's nothing wrong with rebranding. It occurs more and more these days, since things are changing faster and faster.

Remember Kentucky Fried Chicken? Yeah, that's right…the one that's now KFC. They rebranded because consumers became concerned about eating too much fried food (it's loaded with saturated fat.) People started eating healthier, and fried food just wasn't cutting the mustard anymore, so to speak.

So, in an effort to avoid losing market share due to changing tastes, Kentucky Fried Chicken dropped the "Fried" baggage and went with crisp, clean initials, rebranding itself as KFC. They even went so far as to give the Colonel's image a makeover, removing eyebrows and apron and generally sprucing him up. Even better, rumor has it that KFC now claims that it stands for "Kitchen Fresh Chicken." Sounds healthy, right? Same product, new spin. You get the idea.

Other companies have done the same thing. In 2003-2004, the brawny-looking Bounty paper towel man got a makeover. Apparently, the company decided that with the growing ethnic demographics in America, it was time to give their blonde-haired, blue-eyes image dark hair, dark eyes and a slightly swarthier complexion. A similar make-over was performed by the Aunt Jemima syrup makers, who transformed Aunt Jemima's image from an apron-clad servant to an upscale woman who happens to cook.

You don't have to do a global rebrand. If you can afford the resources, you can selectively rebrand for certain markets. McDonald's does this to capture black peoples' business, with commercials that portray "Mickey-D's", complete with a hip-hop soundtrack and a catchy "I'm lovin' it" theme.

Rebranding doesn't always work, however. Two words: New Coke. Of course, that wasn't just rebranding, that was monkeying around with a time-honored formula. But still…before you rebrand, check with your focus groups. Make sure you ask the right questions, like, "If Coke tasted like *this* and came in a can like *that*, would you still buy it?"

64

It is entirely possible to lose even while appearing to win. If you expend a tremendous amount of time, money, and effort to win meager market share, you've caused yourself a net loss.

Sun Tsu said, "Win as easily as picking up a fallen hair. Don't use all your forces." OK, so it's almost never as easy as picking up a piece of your shorn locks after you've had a haircut, but even so, your expansion into a new market should be so well thought-out and well-planned that it feels almost effortless.

You don't need Sun Tsu to tell you not to put all your eggs in one basket, but unfortunately that rule fell by the wayside during the dot-com boom, when tens of thousands put all their money into one start-up. Some had sense enough to cash out early, and they live well. Others…not so good.

There is a time and a season for all things (that's from the Bible, Ecclesiasteces 3:1-8), and you need to develop your sense of timing for when to enter a new market. Don't over-analyze or try to develop pin-point laser accuracy, just be close.

Hear what they say, not what you want to hear

You know what you want your customers and trial markets to say: some variation of "I love it, it's hot, I want to buy 1,000 of 'em!" And when you're predisposed to hearing good news, it's all too easy to misinterpret customer feedback in the most positive light.

Resist that temptation. Keep your mind open. Listen to what customers and focus groups are really telling you. Watch their body language. Keep a lookout for damning with faint praise. Hear what they truly say, not what you want to hear.

Successful marketers aren't necessarily the most well-educated, intelligent marketers in the business. They're just the ones who've learned to pick their battles so that they get a high percentage of wins. They don't rush into a market against a Goliath of a competitor, or when it's the wrong time. They prevent defeat by imagining what could go wrong and planning what they'll do if that happens.

If you prevent yourself from losing, you will win. Set yourself up in "can't lose" markets. What sorts of markets are "can't lose?" Here are a few examples to get your creative juices flowing:

- Captive audiences—people who have to have something, or at least *think* they have to have it, and you're the first in the market. Examples include satellite TV companies who market to rural areas, secured credit cards for those who can't qualify for regular cards, and lower-income housing.

- Emerging new traffic patterns or new suburban malls— if you know that something is going to draw traffic, place yourself near it or on the road to it.

- Any sort of service that lets overworked professionals outsource household tasks such as cleaning, laundry, gourmet cooking, childcare, birthday party prep, you name it.

Everyone always has a blame-game session when a campaign fails, but it would be more productive to have a "what went right" session immediately following a successful campaign. Those lessons-learned might include knowing who works well with whom, which tactics gave the biggest bang for the buck, and so on.

Don't overlook the obvious. Sales people are taught, "Always ask for the order," because most of the advertising you see these days doesn't ask for the order. Much of it is merely brand identification, such as big Nike billboards that show a famous basketball star (you know the one) and say "Just do it," and feature that swoosh logo.

Asking for the order means making it easy for customers to buy from you. And yes, Sun Tsu had something to say about this: "Victory goes to those who make winning easy." Don't make customers have to search for your contact info. If you're running a website, put a link to the order screen on every page.

In particular, invest the time and money in being able to process credit cards seamlessly, especially over the internet. An increasingly large number of people shop that way, so make it easy for them to buy from you. Amazon.com does this with "one-click ordering" for customers who sign up. It's very seductive…click once and that bright, shiny new book or widget will show up at your door soon. Yes, widgets. Amazon was smart enough to ask customers what else they'd like to see Amazon carry, and they've diversified greatly and profited from it.

Expand into markets where you don't have to fight tooth and nail for customers. Rebrand and redefine product categories in such a way that you become the clear leader. Take the Bugaboo stroller, for instance…

The Bugaboo company noticed two important things. One was that professional couples are waiting until later in life to have children, which results in a pair of very well-off parents with high incomes who are upwardly mobile and want everyone to know it. Yep, yuppies with babes, you got it.

The second thing was that these couples snap up every upscale status-symbol version of every product they can get their hands on, from Limited Edition Hummers to expresso

67

machines, to bread bakers, to au pairs imported from France. But—and this is critical—there were no upscale, urban-assault-type baby strollers on the market.

Thus, circa 2005, the edgy, European-styled $500 Bugaboo stroller appeared on the streets of New York City, propelled by women wearing exorbitantly expensive sunglasses and dads in LaCoste shirts and khakis. These people want a top-of-the-line stroller, sure, but they also want every single item they possess to scream, "We're really raking in the big bucks, thank you very much!"

Make sure you identify a winner of a market before you design a campaign, and then make it easy to buy. Look for trends that are converging—that's how the Hummer came to be when military stuff became cool and soccer moms wanted the biggest and best SUV on the market to go pick up a quart of milk—oh, I'm sorry, *organic* milk!

If you get the chance to do an end-run around the competition or out-flank them, don't pass that up. Ever use Snap-On tools? They cost a lot, don't they? About twice as much as the competition. But their service plan is amazing. People will pay more for great service, and that is Snap-On's end run around the competition.

Offering superior service is a great way to command a higher price for your product because it elevates you to a higher niche. Conversely, retailers who compete on price by slashing service to the bone often earn a bad reputation for themselves. I'm not going to name names, but think of any big-box store retailer you've been to because the prices were low. What happens, though, when you try to get some help or return something? It's a disaster, right? Yep, and that's why a certain segment

68

of the market never goes there—they are willing to pay higher prices for great service.

Find your niche, get the right branding, rebrand if necessary, pick your timing, and go for it.

Whew, that was pretty intense stuff, wasn't it? But now you have a better sense of how to use tactics in marketing, which should ultimately increase your bottom line. And what if you could do all that the lazy man or woman's way, with a very efficient use of energy?

In the next chapter, you're going to learn some incredibly powerful ways to take advantage of your competitor's momentum, pull off sneak attacks, make more money by offering better value, and generally become a real pain in the ass to your competitors…which will profit *you*!

69

Action Steps:

1. Think about how you play defense—list 5 ways in which your organization actively prevents loss of market share.

2. List six ways in which you can prevent loss of market share—ways that you're not using right now.

3. Ask 10 customers what else you can help them with and write down their responses. If the same thing is mentioned by at least three of them, get working on it.

4. Consider your branding. Is it time to rebrand? Are there market segments that you could do a selective rebranding for?

5. Write down all the ways you know in which you ask customers for their order. Now think of seven new ways in which you could ask.

6. Think about your customers. Write down their demographics. How are those demographics changing (hint: everything changes)? Now, how can you capitalize on those changes? Are there new needs and wants these customers have, perhaps as a result of trends converging? Solve this puzzle and you might be first in the new market.

ORIGINAL TEXT: Attack by Stratagem

1. *Sun Tzu said: The good fighters of old first put themselves beyond the possibility of defeat, and then waited for an opportunity of defeating the enemy.*

2. *To secure ourselves against defeat lies in our own hands, but the opportunity of defeating the enemy is provided by the enemy himself.*

3. *Thus the good fighter is able to secure himself against defeat, but cannot make certain of defeating the enemy.*

4. *Hence the saying: One may know how to conquer without being able to do it.*

5. *Security against defeat implies defensive tactics; ability to defeat the enemy means taking the offensive.*

6. *Standing on the defensive indicates insufficient strength; attacking, a superabundance of strength.*

7. *The general who is skilled in defense hides in the most secret recesses of the earth; he who is skilled in attack flashes forth from the topmost heights of heaven. Thus on the one hand we have ability to protect ourselves; on the other, a victory that is complete.*

8. *To see victory only when it is within the ken of the common herd is not the acme of excellence.*

9. *Neither is it the acme of excellence if you fight and conquer and the whole Empire says, "Well done!"*

10. To lift an autumn hair is no sign of great strength; to see the sun and moon is no sign of sharp sight; to hear the noise of thunder is no sign of a quick ear.

11. What the ancients called a clever fighter is one who not only wins, but excels in winning with ease.

12. Hence his victories bring him neither reputation for wisdom nor credit for courage.

13. He wins his battles by making no mistakes. Making no mistakes is what establishes the certainty of victory, for it means conquering an enemy that is already defeated.

14. Hence the skillful fighter puts himself into a position which makes defeat impossible, and does not miss the moment for defeating the enemy.

15. Thus it is that in war the victorious strategist only seeks battle after the victory has been won, whereas he who is destined to defeat first fights and afterwards looks for victory.

16. The consummate leader cultivates the moral law, and strictly adheres to method and discipline; thus it is in his power to control success.

17. In respect of military method, we have, firstly, Measurement; secondly, Estimation of quantity; thirdly, Calculation; fourthly, Balancing of chances; fifthly, Victory.

18. *Measurement owes its existence to Earth; Estimation of quantity to Measurement; Calculation to Estimation of quantity; Balancing of chances to Calculation; and Victory to Balancing of chances.*

19. *A victorious army opposed to a routed one, is as a pound's weight placed in the scale against a single grain.*

20. *The onrush of a conquering force is like the bursting of pent-up waters into a chasm a thousand fathoms deep.*

73

Chapter 7

THE EFFICIENCY OF THE LAZY MAN—USE OF ENERGY

Wouldn't it be great if you could capture market share without a lot of work? If you could harness the power of momentum to divert a campaign into a niche and own it? You can! In this chapter, you'll learn how to use your energy so that you get the biggest bang for your bucks.

When you throw significant resources into a campaign, that's using energy. When a campaign's already in motion and you give it a nudge to really amp it up, that's using momentum. It's much easier to keep a cruise ship moving that to overcome the inertia and get it going to start with. Your marketing is no different. Getting your brand out there is the hard part. Selling to people who know your brand is the easy part.

Sun Tsu said, "You fight a large army the same as you fight a small one." Don't let a large market intimidate you—approach it the same way you'd approach a smaller market. Think of Southwest Airlines. They entered the hyper-competitive world of air travel fearlessly, and managed to carve out a niche for themselves as "no frills" by offering only water and peanuts on all flights and doing away with assigned seating and all the bookkeeping hassles it entails.

Making more money with marketing momentum

Ever take a martial arts class? Many of them—Judo, in particular—teach you to use your opponent's size and weight against him. You might be up against a bonafide, 300-pound bad-boy, but once you get him swinging at you, you've made him overcome his initial and considerable inertia. Now he's like a cruise ship in motion, and with a little nudge you can use his own momentum to send him crashing to the ground.

OpenSource is trying to do that to MicroSoft, using MicroSoft's strength in being a large corporation against it. And they just might win…remember Hertz and Avis ("We Try Harder?)

Sneak attacks succeed

Attack when your competition doesn't expect it. When would a retailer not expect any competition? The biggie would be right after Christmas…or used to be, anyhow. Recently, many retailers have jumped into this void by selling gift cards for Christmas, which are then redeemed in January.

Everybody knows the best time to sell your house is in late spring and early summer, when all the families with kids are moving, right? Nope. According to Blake Outlaw of the Outlaw Group of Keller-Williams Realty in Austin, Texas, spring and early summer is when the largest number of homes are placed on the market, and the largest number of buyers are looking.

However, if you look at the ratio of buyers to homes on the market, that ratio is actually higher in mid-January because the number of homes on the market is much smaller, and the number of buyers is less smaller. So the ratio of buyers to homes on the market is actually highest on January 15th, which Outlaw says is the best day to list your home for sale. But, of course, most people don't probe into statistics, they just follow the conventional wisdom…which is neither truly conventional nor is it wise.

Always look for ways in which you can use the element of surprise in your marketing campaigns. Your goal should be to make the competition say, "I never dreamed they'd do *that*!" This is why outrageous publicity stunts, like CEOs bungee-jumping from their buildings, work. It's the element of surprise.

Customers have expectations about how they are marketed to, and they are surprised and delighted when someone sells them something in a new and interesting way. But then, over time, that new and interesting way will become old and boring.

Remember when e-mail first came out? Nobody minded spam back then, because e-mail was such a novelty that we took the time to read everything we got—seriously!

Prior to the 1990's, many customers dreaded buying a new car even though they really wanted the end result. It was the process of haggling, negotiating and backroom deals that annoyed them. General Motors (GM) was smart enough to pick up on this and they launched their Saturn division.

Saturn's marketing edge was a new and interesting (and to many, better) process for buying a car—no haggling, no tirades, no tears, no brother-in-law backroom deals, just one fixed price. People loved it. They loved it enough that Saturn owners began having their own special get-togethers.

Never underestimate the power of surprise.

Sun Tsu said, "There are only a few notes in the scale. Yet you can always mix them. You can never see all the shades of victory." Yeah, Sun Tsu thought there were a lot of songs out there…he had no idea, did he? Yet they all stem from 7 notes, along with some sharps and flats. There really aren't all that many marketing methods, broadly speaking, yet, you can mix and match them any way you like. In fact, it's better if you do.

In the same way, there are just a handful of basic human needs and drives: sustenance, shelter, sex, entertainment, power, and wanting to be liked are a few. But people satisfy those needs in millions of different ways. One guy satisfies his need for power by becoming a CEO. Another buys a Jaguar. Still another gets into bar fights every Saturday night.

Likewise, the values that customers hold dear tend to be fairly simple: people want to be liked, they want to get rich, eat great food, have lots of sex, and they want to laugh and have fun. Non-fiction authors know there are 5 topics that can always be counted on to sell books. They are:

- Diets
- Cookbooks
- How to make money
- Relationships
- How to succeed in business
- And, in America, self-help/recovery books

You've got to hit your customers' hot buttons. Sun Tzu called it, "Making the enemy angry." You don't want to make your customers angry at you, but you might want to tap into their deep frustration at not being able to find a solution for whatever problem they have. You want to make them feel something; you want to touch a nerve.

Sun Tsu advised that you should make the enemy pay dearly. The modern equivalent is creating a niche market that your competitors would have to spend a fortune to get into.

Get more money by offering better value

To get more money for your product, you must firmly establish in your customers' mind the notion that your product is the very best value for the money. This is sometimes called the "boutique" strategy, but it's the best one I know of for commanding higher prices. You can, indeed, get customers to pay more for your products and services than they do for the competitions', but to do that you must create the perception of higher value.

What's higher value? To use the Starbucks model, it's when you can charge $3.00 for a small cup of coffee because it was made from the finest shade-grown Arabica beans on a small, organic co-op farm, hand-roasted, precision ground, and served up in a hip-and-happenin' cup. Take *that*, Folgers!

You could also build your foundation for higher prices with the value of great service. In Austin, Texas, there are chain stores that sell running shoes for $35-$70. Then there is Run-Tex. They sell those same shoes for $50-$150. Run-Tex has a very large and loyal customer base who will wade through hell and high water to buy shoes from them and them alone.

Why? Because Run-Tex...

- Has salespeople who are runners, and they have you take off your shoes, they look at your feet, they ask you what sort of running you do, then they make good recommendations.

79

- Lets you try out running shoes outside on an artificial surface they've installed.

- Accepts donations of old shoes, which they give to charity, and gives you $10 off a new pair.

- Takes back running shoes that didn't work for you.

- Offers free running clinics and classes on Monday, Tuesday, Wednesday, and Thursday evenings, after work.

- Sponsors many races in the area.

- Donates heavily to charity.

Now *that's* good service!

Making the basics work for you

Have you ever gone back to an old textbook and seen something in the very first chapter and thought, "Hey…that's a great idea! I'd forgotten all about that." Marketing can get very complex, very esoteric, and very confusing. But good marketers, like good generals, never lose sight of the basics, which are called that for a reason.

At the very heart of marketing is the time-honored maxim, "Always ask for the order." Sure, it sounds obvious. But you'd be surprised how many times it's left out. The current trend towards brand establishment, with the big Coke and Nike signs that give no product information and don't ask for the order, are a waste of time if you ask me. Ask by saying, "Call now to…" or "Click here to order," or, "So, can I put you down for…"

When you ask for the order, you must always give a deadline. People are so busy these days, they'll put off a purchase they intend to make until they forget about it unless you prod them. However, you must prod them gently and respectfully. It's best if you can give a good reason why the offer is for a limited time only, unless you're McDonalds (and they're big enough to pull it off.)

Make it clear what you are offering, and lead with the benefits to the customer. Far too many tech adds start with specs. People don't buy a stereo system because it has 14" subwoofers with an ABC and an XYZ laser-whatever. They buy a stereo system because it lets them jam large and loud to the beat. Lead with that.

Never make a customer dig down through an ad for info he or she needs to make a purchase decision. Make it easy for them to see what you're offering and to buy it.

There's power in being a pain in the ass

If I could sum up most of Sun Tsu's wisdom, it would be this: be contrary. Do the opposite of what the competition is doing, and do it in the opposite way. If they are:

- Strong—act weak.

- Weak—act strong.

- Decisive—act flaky.

- Indecisive—be decisive.

- Phone orders only—offer online and e-mail ordering

- Using voicemail—have a live person take calls

Get a feel for the way that marketing is going in your area…and then do something entirely different. Use your creativity. Be Saturn. Bring to the market a whole new way of doing things.

Change the game. Make it yours. Own it.

Are you fired up? You should be! Now that you know how to leverage your energy and that of your competitors, you can really get your marketing moving. In the next chapter, I'll show you some great ways to use strength and weakness so that you grab maximum market share. We'll talk about shark-infested waters, and making your competitors divide so that you can conquer!

82

Action Steps

1. Think about a competitor you have who's bigger than you. What's their current campaign about? Now brainstorm on ways in which you can use the power of their large momentum against them (hint: they won't be able to stop or change course as quickly as you.) Divert the market…make marketing about something other than what they're making it about.

2. Consider your next marketing campaign. Write down 5 ways in which you can stealth that puppy right under your competitor's noses. What resources will you need to make it a sneak attack?

3. Write down three of your products or services. Now list five ways in which you could reposition each to be a better value—at a higher price and profit margin—by adding a little extra in the product itself or in your service.

4. Take a look at your current marketing materials. Do you ask for the order? Fix it. Do you have a deadline? Is it clear within one second of looking at your ad what you're selling, what the price is, and how to order now?

5. Think of campaigns you've run. Do they have some consistencies? Have you gotten predictable? What kind of campaign could you design that would have customers and competitors alike saying, "Wow, that's awesome…and we never saw it coming?"

ORIGINAL TEXT: Use of energy

1. *Sun Tzu said: The control of a large force is the same principle as the control of a few men: it is merely a question of dividing up their numbers.*

2. *Fighting with a large army under your command is nowise different from fighting with a small one: it is merely a question of instituting signs and signals.*

3. *To ensure that your whole host may withstand the brunt of the enemy's attack and remain unshaken— this is effected by maneuvers direct and indirect.*

4. *That the impact of your army may be like a grind-stone dashed against an egg—this is effected by the science of weak points and strong.*

5. *In all fighting, the direct method may be used for joining battle, but indirect methods will be needed in order to secure victory.*

6. *Indirect tactics, efficiently applied, are inex-haustible as Heaven and Earth, unending as the flow of rivers and streams; like the sun and moon, they end but to begin anew; like the four seasons, they pass away to return once more.*

7. *There are not more than five musical notes, yet the combinations of these five give rise to more melodies than can ever be heard.*

84

8. *There are not more than five primary colors (blue, yellow, red, white, and black), yet in combination they produce more hues than can ever been seen.*

9. *There are not more than five cardinal tastes (sour, acrid, salt, sweet, bitter), yet combinations of them yield more flavors than can ever be tasted.*

10. *In battle, there are not more than two methods of attack—the direct and the indirect; yet these two in combination give rise to an endless series of maneuvers.*

11. *The direct and the indirect lead on to each other in turn. It is like moving in a circle—you never come to an end. Who can exhaust the possibilities of their combination?*

85

12. *The onset of troops is like the rush of a torrent which will even roll stones along in its course.*

13. *The quality of decision is like the well-timed swoop of a falcon which enables it to strike and destroy its victim.*

14. *Therefore the good fighter will be terrible in his onset, and prompt in his decision.*

15. *Energy may be likened to the bending of a crossbow; decision, to the releasing of a trigger.*

16. *Amid the turmoil and tumult of battle, there may be seeming disorder and yet no real disorder at all; amid confusion and chaos, your array may be without head or tail, yet it will be proof against defeat.*

17. Simulated disorder postulates perfect discipline, simulated fear postulates courage; simulated weakness postulates strength.

18. Hiding order beneath the cloak of disorder is simply a question of subdivision; concealing courage under a show of timidity presupposes a fund of latent energy; masking strength with weakness is to be effected by tactical dispositions.

19. Thus one who is skillful at keeping the enemy on the move maintains deceitful appearances, according to which the enemy will act. He sacrifices something, that the enemy may snatch at it.

20. By holding out baits, he keeps him on the march; then with a body of picked men he lies in wait for him.

21. The clever combatant looks to the effect of combined energy, and does not require too much from individuals. Hence his ability to pick out the right men and utilize combined energy.

22. When he utilizes combined energy, his fighting men become as it were like unto rolling logs or stones. For it is the nature of a log or stone to remain motionless on level ground, and to move when on a slope; if four-cornered, to come to a standstill, but if round-shaped, to go rolling down.

23. Thus the energy developed by good fighting men is as the momentum of a round stone rolled down a mountain thousands of feet in height. So much on the subject of energy.

Chapter 8

LEVERAGING YOUR STRENGTH TO CAPTURE MARKET SHARE—WEAK POINTS AND STRONG

E ver heard that there's weakness in strength, or strength in weakness? No, it's not just a nonsensical paradox. That old thing about the sturdy oak tree and the willow weed illustrates it perfectly. The oak tree's strength doomed it in the storm, since it was too strong too bend. The willow's weakness—they bend easily—was its strength.

In this chapter, you'll learn how to use the incredible power of customer weaknesses to put yourself—and your bottom line—in a superior position of strength.

Sun Tsu said that the stronger army is the one who storms through empty terrain, or into an empty battlefield. An army that moves into an area that's already occupied isn't so strong…or won't be for very long.

The modern marketing version of this is a customer need. That's weakness. Strength is the satisfying of that need. It may sound simple, but there are many nuances involved.

First to market is first to cash a paycheck

Your goal should be to get into a market before your competition does. When you can do that, you've put yourself in the driver's seat and you're strong. Conversely, avoid entering markets with entrenched competition. You don't want to go up against Coke in the common soda market, Xerox in the photocopier business, Kleenex in the tissue business…you get the idea.

There's a big exception, though. If you can manage to rebrand an existing product, or carve out a niche that didn't exist before, go for it. That's what Starbucks did. If they hadn't created a gourmet coffee and coffeehouse niche, they'd have been stupid to enter the crowded coffee market against the likes of Folgers and Eight O'Clock. So they did an end-run around the coffee giants, carving off a big enough niche that it's become a full-scale market.

And John Mackey is the kind of man who can carve out a local niche and turn it into a large national corporation. Whole Foods Market (WFM) began as a small health-food store in Austin, Texas, in the '70's. Right from the start, founder Mackey realized that WFM wasn't competing against Safeway, HEB, or other area grocery stores. The potential clients for WFM were health-conscious consumers who shied away from the pesticide-laden produce and hormone-filled meats of conventional grocery stores.

The leap from health-food store to classy, upscale organic store came when Mackey realized one more thing about his customers: they were doing quite well financially, and were willing to spend more on healthier food and drink. Thus, the concept of the Whole Foods Market evolved into what we see today— hip, trendy, and oh-so-good for you.

Swim in shark-infested waters where competitors won't

To get a market all to yourself, consider entering risky markets. Most companies are very risk-averse and they won't follow

88

you unless and until you build up a substantial customer base (i.e, until you prove it's safe.) By then, of course, you are the one who's entrenched in that market and they'd have to violate a cardinal Sun Tsu rule to enter that market.

Risky markets can pay off—the trick is in finding the optimum risk-to-reward ratio. I knew a real estate investor who was very successful with low-income properties that catered to minimum-wage earners. There was never a dull moment at those places. There were shootings, a few murders, more domestic disputes than anyone bothered to count, doors kicked in…and yet, my friend made it pay.

How? Well, there were several ways. He:

- Charged the highest security deposit the law would allow, because the odds were there would be damage.

- Charged the highest rate the market would bear, and got it by offering better and friendlier service than competing landlords did.

- Spent the bare minimum on fix-ups and repairs. I'm not going to call him a slumlord, but I will say that he did the minimum necessary to keep things working and up to code. New carpet and paint went in every 5 years instead of every 3, and landscaping was left to the tenant. In other words, he kept production costs low.

Another good strategy is to enter a market that has a barrier to entry, if you have a way past the barrier. If you're flush with cash, consider entering a market that requires considerable advertising with a worthwhile payoff. If you're a citizen of some country that only gives helping-hand grants to its citizens, use that. If the market is a minority community that distrusts outsiders, yet you have a member of that community on your staff, go for it.

Find the unfulfilled need and fill it

There's also something to be said for stirring up trouble deep within your customers. What the heck is that? Well, it's when your marketing nudges them out of their comfort zone. You create a need or want where there wasn't one before. Car companies have elevated this to a fine art—most people don't budget $20,000+ for a new car every 4 years or so, yet they are seduced by the sexy sizzle of the car ads on TV and in magazines.

You don't have to create a need out of nothing. If you look hard enough and ask enough questions, you can discover needs that are being only partially fulfilled by your competitors. One example is the addition of cup holders and map pockets to cars, trucks and SUV's.

Thirty years ago, people balanced coffee cups or sodas on dashboards and stuck maps between seats. Coffee got spilled, maps got lost. Then several entrepreneurs saw that these customers had needs that were being only partially fulfilled by the car companies—the cars got them where they were going, but didn't hold mugs, cups or maps. Soon little plastic gadgets began popping up in auto supply stores. These gadgets latched onto the inside of the driver's door and held a cup.

Car companies took notice and started quizzing customers on what else they'd like in their cars, and now we have vehicles loaded with backseat TV's, seat warmers, and satellite radios.

Never assume you know your customer's needs. Ask them what they think and what else they'd like to see in your product or service. Do this on a regular basis. Don't let your customer's needs go unfulfilled, or partially-fulfilled. If you do, someone else will take care of them.

Find a need and fill it. And while you're at it, take a good look at how your competitors are filling those needs…or not. Have they overlooked a market segment, or decided it's too much trouble? Before you rush in, do your homework. Some customers are indeed more trouble than their worth, but you should be the one to decide that—not your competitors.

When they divide, you conquer

Have your competitors divided their attention, leaving a certain market segment under-served? American cell phone companies unknowingly did this in 2005, when they moved from analog networks to digital so that people could take cell phones anywhere in the world and use them. However, many users were angry about this shift because even though digital gave them many more bells and whistles on their phones, sound quality decreased.

The reason it decreased is because digital technology is constantly translating, coding, and reassembling your voice, whereas analog simply translates sound into electrical impulses continuously. Thus, there is a market niche right now for cell phones using analog technology. Not all consumers travel overseas, and an increasing number of them are becoming very price-conscious.

Better yet, if you can subtly encourage your competitors to diversify into many markets and spread themselves too thin, you can then swoop in to offer superior service to the segments they ignore. Any company that tries to be all things to all markets segments is going to gloss over a niche here and there. Try to make your competitors do this. Then, find the overlooked and under-served niches. This works especially well when the other guy tries to be a global player.

Another wonderful tactic is misdirection. Sun Tzu was quite fond of it. Watch what your competitors focus on. Too much focus on quality makes them a target for you on price. Too much focus on price makes them vulnerable on the quality front. If they zero in on speed, they will lose accuracy. Focusing on accuracy slows them down.

When a company tries to be all things to all people, they overlook specialty markets. Whole Foods Market recognized this. Focusing on selling to big companies makes you overlook selling to small companies. You can overlook small companies by selling to households and individuals.

If the competition is much bigger than you are, avoid competing with them directly on their turf. Know the strengths and weaknesses not only of your company, but of your marketing plan. Don't try to be all things to all people. Be selective.

Be the innovator, not the "us, too" company. Don't tell everything you know…let people wonder. Keep your mouth shut about your target market and instruct your people to do likewise. Your competitors should only find out what your target market was after you have captured it. And even then, they should be clueless about how you did what you did.

After you've captured a market, stay on top of it. People's needs are very fluid these days, so make sure you keep your finger on their pulse. And keep your market positioning fluid. Be like an ancient Chinese army…ready to shift at any time.

I know that's a lot to take in for one chapter, but it's important that as a Samurai of modern marketing, you know how to fully leverage your strength to take advantage of customer and competitor weakness. After all, you need the right weapons to go to war.

In the next chapter, we're going to jump from the frying pan straight into the fire of 21st century marketing. You'll learn how to profit from meeting customers where they are and I'll show you how to become a zen master of production and distribution such that they work for you, not the other way around.

93

Action Steps

1. Recall a time when you or your company was first in a market. If the results were not hugely successful, why not? Now brainstorm, and come up with a market that you could be first into.

2. Think of markets that you and your competitors shy away from because they're considered dangerous. What is it that's dangerous about them? Is there a way you could minimize the risk and run a profitable marketing campaign?

3. Is there a potential market you're avoiding because there is a barrier to entry? How might you gain the resources to overcome that barrier?

4. Think about one of your competitor's marketing strategies. Is there a market they are under-serving? Are they truly filling all the customers' needs? Look for a market that is only being partially served, then make a plan to fully serve it.

5. In what ways can you encourage your competitors to over-extend themselves? Do you have a competitor right now who's in the middle of an expansion? Have they neglected a market segment that you could capture?

ORIGINAL TEXT: Weak Points and Strong

1. *Sun Tzu said: Whoever is first in the field and awaits the coming of the enemy, will be fresh for the fight; whoever is second in the field and has to hasten to battle will arrive exhausted.*

2. *Therefore the clever combatant imposes his will on the enemy, but does not allow the enemy's will to be imposed on him.*

3. *By holding out advantages to him, he can cause the enemy to approach of his own accord; or, by inflicting damage, he can make it impossible for the enemy to draw near.*

4. *If the enemy is taking his ease, he can harass him; if well supplied with food, he can starve him out; if quietly encamped, he can force him to move.*

5. *Appear at points which the enemy must hasten to defend; march swiftly to places where you are not expected.*

6. *An army may march great distances without distress, if it marches through country where the enemy is not.*

7. *You can be sure of succeeding in your attacks if you only attack places which are undefended. You can ensure the safety of your defense if you only hold positions that cannot be attacked.*

8. Hence that general is skillful in attack whose opponent does not know what to defend; and he is skillful in defense whose opponent does not know what to attack.

9. O divine art of subtlety and secrecy! Through you we learn to be invisible, through you inaudible; and hence we can hold the enemy's fate in our hands.

10. You may advance and be absolutely irresistible, if you make for the enemy's weak points; you may retire and be safe from pursuit if your movements are more rapid than those of the enemy.

11. If we wish to fight, the enemy can be forced to an engagement even though he be sheltered behind a high rampart and a deep ditch. All we need do is attack some other place that he will be obliged to relieve.

12. If we do not wish to fight, we can prevent the enemy from engaging us even though the lines of our encampment be merely traced out on the ground. All we need do is to throw something odd and unaccountable in his way.

13. By discovering the enemy's dispositions and remaining invisible ourselves, we can keep our forces concentrated, while the enemy's must be divided.

14. We can form a single united body, while the enemy must split up into fractions. Hence there will be a whole pitted against separate parts of a whole, which means that we shall be many to the enemy's few.

15. And if we are able thus to attack an inferior force with a superior one, our opponents will be in dire straits.

16. The spot where we intend to fight must not be made known; for then the enemy will have to prepare against a possible attack at several different points; and his forces being thus distributed in many directions, the numbers we shall have to face at any given point will be proportionately few.

17. For should the enemy strengthen his van, he will weaken his rear; should he strengthen his rear, he will weaken his van; should he strengthen his left, he will weaken his right; should he strengthen his right, he will weaken his left. If he sends reinforcements everywhere, he will everywhere be weak.

18. Numerical weakness comes from having to prepare against possible attacks; numerical strength, from compelling our adversary to make these preparations against us.

19. Knowing the place and the time of the coming battle, we may concentrate from the greatest distances in order to fight.

20. But if neither time nor place be known, then the left wing will be impotent to succor the right, the right equally impotent to succor the left, the van unable to relieve the rear, or the rear to support the van. How much more so if the furthest portions of

the army are anything under a hundred LI apart, and even the nearest are separated by several LI!

21. *Though according to my estimate the soldiers of Yueh exceed our own in number, that shall advantage them nothing in the matter of victory. I say then that victory can be achieved.*

22. *Though the enemy be stronger in numbers, we may prevent him from fighting. Scheme so as to discover his plans and the likelihood of their success.*

23. *Rouse him, and learn the principle of his activity or inactivity. Force him to reveal himself, so as to find out his vulnerable spots.*

24. *Carefully compare the opposing army with your own, so that you may know where strength is superabundant and where it is deficient.*

25. *In making tactical dispositions, the highest pitch you can attain is to conceal them; conceal your dispositions, and you will be safe from the prying of the subtlest spies, from the machinations of the wisest brains.*

26. *How victory may be produced for them out of the enemy's own tactics—that is what the multitude cannot comprehend.*

27. *All men can see the tactics whereby I conquer, but what none can see is the strategy out of which victory is evolved.*

28. *Do not repeat the tactics which have gained you one victory, but let your methods be regulated by the infinite variety of circumstances.*

29. *Military tactics are like unto water; for water in its natural course runs away from high places and hastens downwards.*

30. *So in war, the way is to avoid what is strong and to strike at what is weak.*

31. *Water shapes its course according to the nature of the ground over which it flows; the soldier works out his victory in relation to the foe whom he is facing.*

32. *Therefore, just as water retains no constant shape, so in warfare there are no constant conditions.*

33. *He who can modify his tactics in relation to his opponent and thereby succeed in winning, may be called a heaven-born captain.*

34. *The five elements (water, fire, wood, metal, earth) are not always equally predominant; the four seasons make way for each other in turn. There are short days and long; the moon has its periods of waning and waxing.*

99

Chapter 9

HOW TO PRODUCE PEAK PROFITS WITH MASTERFUL MANEUVERING— MANEUVERING AN ARMY

H ave you ever been told not to show-off, to stop bragging, to quit hamming it up? You didn't listen, I hope. Good, because you need to showboat in marketing. In this chapter, I'll explain why and how, and I'll show you the ancient Chinese art of deflecting a dull problem into a glittering opportunity. Read on…

Sun Tzu must have had the modern corporation in mind when he said, in so many words, "In war, the general receives his commands from the sovereign. After putting together an army and concentrating his forces, the general must blend and harmonize the different elements before he makes camp. After that comes tactical maneuvering, and there's nothing more difficult."

Newsflash from the 21st century: it's only difficult if you haven't read the information I'm about to share with you. Modern generals have said, "No battle plan survives contact with the enemy," and that's what I'm going to help you with. What do you do when the shit hits the fan in the middle of a marketing campaign and you must adapt or die?

If you're made of the right stuff, failure isn't an option—you adapt. Read on, and you'll learn how.

Like war, marketing is expensive and risky. To reduce the degree of risk, you need all the bargaining chips you can get, like timing and a superior product. Look for ways you can leverage what you have and what you are. Remember the Avis "We Try Harder" campaign I talked about earlier? Avis leveraged the fact that they were number two in the rental car industry and turned it into a plus by convincing consumers that it made them try harder.

In war, if a supply route doesn't work, armies find another or forage off of the land. Your equivalent is distribution channels. If they're not working for you, get another or work off of your competitor's distributors.

Profit from meeting customers where they are

When you launch your campaign, positioning is key. Don't make customers have to look for you. Be where they're looking; get right out in front of them. The soda companies figured this out early on. At first, sodas were in stores. After several years of hearing gas station owners report that customers were saying, "Gee, an ice-cold Coke would taste great right now after that long drive," the soda companies started selling to gas station owners.

Those owners would put sodas in horse troughs filled with ice and water and sell them for 5 cents. When that proved popular, the soda companies invented vending machines. Now Coke sells at least as many sodas—if not more—from machines as from stores. Vending machines are an excellent example of putting your product in front of the customer.

People who wouldn't take the time to go into a grocery store, pick up a Coke, and stand in line to pay for it will buy a Coke if the machine is right there at the pool, the Laundromat, in the break room, or downstairs in a hotel.

Don't try to make customers come to you—they won't do it. If at all possible, go to them. Remember: we live in the age of convenience. All sorts of goods and services are being brought to consumer's doorsteps. There are:

- Car windshield repair businesses that will come to your home or office.

- Mobile veterinarians who make house calls to your dog or cat.

- Personal chefs who take care of all the shopping, bring the groceries to your home, cook a gourmet meal for your family and then box up and label the left-overs for you.

103

It's good to be ahead of your time, but don't try to launch before your customers are ready. If you do, you risk over-exposure and you've wasted money. Don't market until you've got the product or service ready to roll out. This mistake is made frequently in the computer industry, so much so that the pejorative term for heavily-hyped software that doesn't exist (except for some notes on a techies cocktail napkin) is "vapor-ware."

Semiconductor equipment companies, who make the machines that make computer chips, are particularly guilty of this. They'll listen carefully to a customer, figure out what his wildest dream is, and promise him the moon by next Thursday. Then they go home and break the news to the engineering department that they need to hurry up and design the moon because "We've already sold eight of them." This phenomenon has been made fun of mercilessly in the Dilbert comic strip by Scott Adams.

Don't sell something you haven't designed yet.

Profit from dynamic distribution and powerful production

It's always a delicate balance trying to get into a market. If you go too fast, you'll be first in the market and that's great. But you might not have enough product on hand (remember the techies in an earlier chapter, the ones whose smiles turned to frowns when the number of internet sales reached five digits?) Being unable to fill orders is downright embarrassing and it's difficult to recover from.

104

The alternative, though, is every bit as bad—you make sure your product is there and your distribution is all set up, but then that means you're a "me-too" by the time you hit the market. Not good.

My suggestion is to optimize product or service design, distribution, and market launch by making sure that all of them are flexible and can be changed on the fly if necessary. Source alternate suppliers and distributors that you can use if you need them. As much as possible, build a distribution network that meshes well with your campaign. Budweiser did this in the early days with Clydesdale-pulled delivery wagons, and it made such an impression that those wagons are still used to day as a branded Budweiser symbol.

No distribution network is every perfect. Learn the ins and outs of yours and where the potential is for trouble. Logistics, in particular, can be a big headache—find someone who specializes in taming them and hire him or her.

When you brand, conceal what you're doing from the competition as long as possible. Do what you can to control what they see and perceive about your product. Brand in such a way that your customers notice you but you fly right under the radar of your competitors. Get your name out there in your target market, and ask for the orders.

If you're in a big, diverse market, use lots of different distributors to reach every segment of it. That way, you don't to stress about distribution, just delivery.

Don't hesitate to showboat

Marketing isn't for the timid. There are a ton of ads out there right now. We live in the age of information overload, and your message is competing with thousands of others for people's attention. And even when you do get their attention, you won't have it for very long.

105

To get people to notice you, you need to be edgy, innovative, creative, and a little bit outrageous. Remember the Apple Computer "Think different" posters? They drew the ire of English teachers and editors everywhere, since proper grammar is "think differently." But they got noticed because they were inspiring. And because of that big grammar dust-up.

When you put a new idea out there, don't orphan it. Tie it into something familiar, and unify them to send one clear message. Follow the fiction writer's dictum: make them laugh, make them cry, but make them feel something. Create excitement and a feeling of anticipation. The Burma Shave company did this in the early part of the 20th century with road signs.

You'd be driving along and see a road sign with three words, then another with the next four words, and so on until you'd read a catchy little jingle written on seven or eight consecutive signs. People loved it because it created excitement and antici- pation. This is why multi-message campaigns with teasers work.

Put your strongest ad in the market first, when customer resistance is highest because they don't know you yet. As they get to know your name and brand, resistance withers. When people make a buying decision, they need some validation that they're making the right choice. Your job at that point—late in the campaign—is to give them a sense of safety and security.

Transform problems into opportunities

Don't think for one minute that your campaign is exempt from the effects of the insidious and omnipresent Mr. Murphy. He's always there, looking for things he can and will make go wrong. When he puts in an appearance, don't let it stress you out. See it as an opportunity to hone your coping skills, or to redefine your marketing slant.

Keep a positive outlook among your staff and most espe- cially with your customers. If something has happened to tar- nish your marketing image, remember that people have a short attention span these days and let that work for you by being patient. They'll get over it.

Avoid creating problems for yourself by refraining from entering markets where the competition is strong, solid, and entrenched. There is plenty of opportunity elsewhere.

If your market research shows that your target market has strong opinions or prejudices one way, don't try to change them. You will only make yourself disliked. When someone hates strawberry ice cream, don't feature it—push chocolate, butter pecan, or peppermint instead.

Offer an alternative to something that's gotten tiresome, boring and stale. Make it easy for customers to buy from you by giving them the options and choices they want, both in the product and in how they buy. Increasing numbers of people are buying as much as possible over the internet. Don't make those people pick up the phone, go to a store, or mail in a form—have a website with easy click-click ordering.

And never, every pressure a customer into buying. Lead that horse to water, and he'll drink. Make the customer feel like it's his decision, and a very wise one at that, to buy from you. If you can stroke his self-esteem that way, he'll come back again and again to buy from you.

Did you absorb all that? Great stuff, isn't it? You're going to get some incredible results from that next campaign when you put yourself right out in front of customers so that they can't miss you, aren't you? Sure! And when you fine-tune your distribution and production so that you're in the market early with the ability to deliver, magic will happen.

In the next chapter, you'll learn how Murphy's Law can be successfully broken by staying flexible and discovering the true personality of your markets. I'll discuss playing good defense for profit preservation, how to win new customers with tactics, and how to keep from making 5 deadly mistakes that can spell doom.

Action Steps

1. Think about where your marketing and delivery is. Do you truly meet the customers where they are? Think of three ways or places in which you could position your product so that you would be closer to the customer and increase his or her likelihood of buying.

2. Take a good hard look at your production line and your distribution channels. Are they appropriate for the campaign you're running? If not, how could you change or tweak them? Now think about the next campaign. What would be the ideal production system and distribution network? What will it take to get there?

3. What are four audacious, outrageous things you could do in your marketing that would make customers notice your product in a positive way? What's keeping you from implementing them?

4. Identify 3 problem areas right now in your marketing. Now brainstorm on each one to determine the underlying opportunity. Make a plan to capture at least one of those opportunities.

ORIGINAL TEXT: Maneuvering an Army

1. Sun Tzu said: In war, the general receives his commands from the sovereign.

2. Having collected an army and concentrated his forces, he must blend and harmonize the different elements thereof before pitching his camp.

3. After that, comes tactical maneuvering, than which there is nothing more difficult. The difficulty of tactical maneuvering consists in turning the devious into the direct, and misfortune into gain.

4. Thus, to take a long and circuitous route, after enticing the enemy out of the way, and though starting after him, to contrive to reach the goal before him, shows knowledge of the artifice of DEVIATION.

5. Maneuvering with an army is advantageous; with an undisciplined multitude, most dangerous.

6. If you set a fully equipped army in march in order to snatch an advantage, the chances are that you will be too late. On the other hand, to detach a flying column for the purpose involves the sacrifice of its baggage and stores.

7. Thus, if you order your men to roll up their buff-coats, and make forced marches without halting day or night, covering double the usual distance at a stretch, doing a hundred LI in order to wrest an advantage, the leaders of all your three divisions will fall into the hands of the enemy.

8. The stronger men will be in front, the jaded ones will fall behind, and on this plan only one-tenth of your army will reach its destination.

9. If you march fifty LI in order to outmaneuver the enemy, you will lose the leader of your first division, and only half your force will reach the goal.

10. If you march thirty LI with the same object, two-thirds of your army will arrive.

11. We may take it then that an army without its baggage-train is lost; without provisions it is lost; without bases of supply it is lost.

12. We cannot enter into alliances until we are acquainted with the designs of our neighbors.

13. We are not fit to lead an army on the march unless we are familiar with the face of the country—its mountains and forests, its pitfalls and precipices, its marshes and swamps.

14. We shall be unable to turn natural advantage to account unless we make use of local guides.

15. In war, practice dissimulation, and you will succeed.

16. Whether to concentrate or to divide your troops, must be decided by circumstances.

17. Let your rapidity be that of the wind, your compactness that of the forest.

18. In raiding and plundering be like fire, is immovability like a mountain.

19. *Let your plans be dark and impenetrable as night, and when you move, fall like a thunderbolt.*

20. *When you plunder a countryside, let the spoil be divided amongst your men; when you capture new territory, cut it up into allotments for the benefit of the soldiery.*

21. *Ponder and deliberate before you make a move.*

22. *He will conquer who has learnt the artifice of deviation. Such is the art of maneuvering.*

23. *The Book of Army Management says: On the field of battle, the spoken word does not carry far enough: hence the institution of gongs and drums. Nor can ordinary objects be seen clearly enough: hence the institution of banners and flags.*

24. *Gongs and drums, banners and flags, are means whereby the ears and eyes of the host may be focused on one particular point.*

25. *The host thus forming a single united body, is it impossible either for the brave to advance alone, or for the cowardly to retreat alone. This is the art of handling large masses of men.*

26. *In night-fighting, then, make much use of signal-fires and drums, and in fighting by day, of flags and banners, as a means of influencing the ears and eyes of your army.*

27. *A whole army may be robbed of its spirit; a commander-in-chief may be robbed of his presence of mind.*

111

28. Now a soldier's spirit is keenest in the morning; by noonday it has begun to flag; and in the evening, his mind is bent only on returning to camp.

29. A clever general, therefore, avoids an army when its spirit is keen, but attacks it when it is sluggish and inclined to return. This is the art of studying moods.

30. Disciplined and calm, to await the appearance of disorder and hubbub amongst the enemy:—this is the art of retaining self-possession.

31. To be near the goal while the enemy is still far from it, to wait at ease while the enemy is toiling and struggling, to be well-fed while the enemy is famished:—this is the art of husbanding one's strength.

32. To refrain from intercepting an enemy whose banners are in perfect order, to refrain from attacking an army drawn up in calm and confident array:—this is the art of studying circumstances.

33. It is a military axiom not to advance uphill against the enemy, nor to oppose him when he comes downhill.

34. Do not pursue an enemy who simulates flight; do not attack soldiers whose temper is keen.

35. Do not swallow bait offered by the enemy. Do not interfere with an army that is returning home.

36. When you surround an army, leave an outlet free. Do not press a desperate foe too hard.

37. Such is the art of warfare.

Chapter 10:

HOW TO OUTWIT YOUR OPPONENTS BY SURFING THE WAVE OF CHANGE— VARIATION OF TACTICS

C hange happens. Always has, always will. And in the 21st century, the rate of change is increasing. What do you do when you launch a great campaign and right in the middle of it local events or a change in demographics changes everything? You'll learn the million-dollar answers in this chapter.

There's an old story from West Point that the safest answer that a student of military tactics can give is: "It depends on the conditions and the terrain." Market conditions are always changing, and there is no stock answer on what to do when that happens. Your tactics will depend on the situation, the conditions, and the terrain (meaning the market itself.)

Therefore, one of your strategies should be to learn to read the situation, stay in touch with conditions, and keep your finger on the pulse of the market. You can't adapt to changing conditions if you don't know what they are or which way the wind is blowing.

If market conditions are just piss-poor right at that moment, move on to something else. Remember Lisa, the talking Apple personal computer? She was a big flop because, it turned out, the mar-

113

ket just wasn't ready for a full-blown talking computer in the early 1980's. It took an easing-in process that started with sound effects for certain processes, and later, the development of voice recognition systems for consumers to accept talking computers.

Stay as flexible as possible

What would you do to make a million dollars in profits from your product? Almost anything? Then keep that in mind when things start changing in the course of your marketing campaign. You have options you don't even know about. Some of them are:

- Rebranding your product (the KFC strategy)

- Forging an alliance with a supplier, distributor, or competitor

- Turning a negative into a positive (the Avis "We May Be Number 2, But We Try Harder" strategy)

- Getting creative (the Apple "Think Different" strategy)

- Breaking some rules (sending out targeted emails doesn't have to be SPAM)

If the market goes south after you've entered it and conditions become hopelessly horrible, cut your losses by bailing out so that you preserve resources with which to fight another day. A few stock brokerages had sense enough to do this after the market crashed in 2000, and they have recovered.

Charles Schwab, in particular, has clearly engaged the services of some focus groups and found that people's biggest complaints about traditional brokerages are that—with the advent of the internet—the brokers don't know much more than the buyers. The biggest complaint about discount brokerages is that customers can't get advice. Thus, the "Call Chuck" campaign was born.

Don't try to change the market. Think of the market as a rapid on a large river, and yourself and your marketing team as the crew of a raft. You can't change the rapid, but if you've taken the time to develop your skills, you can change what the rapid does to you. You can avoid getting flipped over and have a really fun time if you can work together to spot the right line, make the right moves and adapt.

In the rushing rapid of market conditions, be the savvy team on the raft that threads its way down, upright, having great fun the whole time. Don't be the argumentative team who can't decide what to do and thus gets their raft tumped over right at the beginning, which leads to an unpleasant swim through rocks and whitewater.

Discover the market's personality

Every market has its quirks, along with its unique strengths and weaknesses. One strength of the current 18-25 market is that they share information with each other through text messaging, cell phone calls, and email to an unprecedented extent. If you can hook some of them, you can get a positive buzz going about your product.

A weakness of that market is that they have a short attention span. They may all talk about how great your product is, but by next week they're on to something new.

Different markets have different personalities. You need to discover what your market's personality is. Are they bombarded with information daily? Then they'll need multiple exposures to your product. Are they put off by a hard sell? Then you'll need to build rapport with them first.

Some markets have already had their personalities defined, but it's often profitable to test-drive those definitions on a focus group. Women, for instance, are assumed to be more emotional than men and thus more vulnerable to touchy-feely marketing that plays on emotions. However, car salespeople have found that when women come into a show room, they are more practical-minded than men, who may let ego drive their buying decision.

Take the time to find out your markets hopes, fears, wants, needs, and above all, heart's desires. Don't be afraid to take a different approach.

Keep what you've fought for with a good defense

When things are going well and you've built up a terrific network of suppliers, distributors, dealers and customers, you need to focus on hanging onto what you have. That's called playing good defense. The Caterpillar tractor company probably didn't realize they were doing it when they set up all those dealerships and treated their customers right. But over the course of the 1990's, they appreciated what they'd done.

What happened? A Japanese tractor, Komatsu, decided to jump into the American market, surround Caterpillar on all fronts, and undercut them on price. After all, they reasoned, that strategy was working very well in the automotive markets for Japanese car-makers…why not tractors?

What Komatsu didn't count on was the tremendous customer loyalty that Caterpillar had built up by doing the right thing time after time. Most customers were willing to pay more for a tractor that they knew was solid quality, and they also knew that if there was a problem, the local Caterpillar dealer would make it right, on the spot.

There was, however, a segment of the market that was attracted to Komatsu because of low prices. In response, Caterpillar became much more efficient in their design process, their manufacturing, their distribution, and in their service—all without sacrificing the quality of product and service they were known for.

Caterpillar won. They won because they knew their market: honest, rural folk who were extremely loyal to businesses that treated them right. And they won because they played good defense.

Win over customers with tactics

Once you've learned as much as you can about your market's unique personality, you can position your product as the solution to their needs and wants. This is the classic tactic used for women's products...just put it in pastel colors, or put a floral pattern on it, and women will buy it. That's not always true, but sometimes it works.

To get them to buy from you, you need to make them think about their problems, make them a little bit uncomfortable, build up their sense of frustration such that they've just got to find a solution. Then you step in as savior and offer them unique benefits they can't find anywhere else.

It's key to use your resources wisely, because like the old song goes, "It don't come easy." You won't win customers without overcoming their resistance—it just doesn't happen. There is no free lunch. Be prepared for the reaction, "Huh...XYX, Inc. Who are *they*, and why are they in my mailbox?"

117

As I said earlier, put your strongest message out there first, when resistance is highest. Tell customers the biggest benefits they'll receive from having your product or service. Don't lead with a long, boring list of technical specifications. That comes last. First, tell that customer what you can do for him.

If you're selling cell phones and service plans, start out by promising the customer he'll never miss an important call again, and only later go into all the little bells and whistles on the phone and how many minutes per month each plan offers.

Your customer sees your ad and he or she thinks one thing: "What's in it for me?" So lead with the biggest benefit to the customer.

You will encounter resistance. Plan for it. Never assume it won't be there. Prepare for worst-case scenarios. Along the same lines, never trust that your competitors are too ethical to go negative on you. They will do it, and they'll do it an precisely the worst time for you, if they're good students of Sun Tzu themselves.

Instead, be prepared for your competitors to go negative on you. Politicians routinely do that today—study their debates and comebacks and you'll see they're always prepared for an attack. Better yet, brand your products in such a way as to make them as attack-proof as possible.

Protect yourself from the 5 killer mistakes

We're all human and we all make mistakes. Often, after you've spend weeks or months planning a campaign, you're so close to it you can't see what people on the outside see. For instance, a local lobbyist who was overworked and tired once sent out an email to 50,000 people, urging them to vote for a candidate referred to only by name. In a town of 100 people, that might work. But not in Austin, Texas...

There are 5 killer mistakes that marketers are prone to make, and most of them stem from ego and hubris. They are:

1. Being OK with losing some customers. If your attitude towards losing customers is "win some, lose some" and you shrug, you will lose customers. It's that simple. The solution? Draw a line in the sand and declare that it is unacceptable to lose customers.

2. Not being brave enough. If you make this mistake, you'll shy away from risky or dangerous markets. The solution is to have some huevos and go for it. Use a role model if you have to, but get up your nerve.

3. Being too prone to anger or other overreaction. If this is your flaw, then people will find that they can provoke you. And then you'll mess up. Do what you need to do to keep your cool. Take yoga classes, get a massage, or just blow off steam playing sports.

4. Falling in love with your products. This is when your products become like your children and you can't look at them objectively. At that point, you've got a big, honking blind spot and you can't make rational decisions.

5. Opening yourself up to public critique. This can be good or bad, but realize that you risk public humiliation when you do it.

As with all other things, you must know yourself, in addition to the market. You have unique strengths, weaknesses, and vulnerabilities. Know what they are and where they are so that

119

you can fully leverage your strength, shore up your weaknesses, and protect your vulnerabilities.

Wow, that's pretty heavy stuff, isn't it? Now you can surf on top of the waves of change, instead of being dragged under them and drowned. Your key coping strategies are staying flexible, discovering the market's personality, playing good defense, winning customers with tactics, and avoiding the big 5 mistakes.

In the next chapter, I'll share with you some valuable strategy for getting top dollar for your products...

Action Steps

1. Recall a time when a marketing campaign didn't do as well as it could have because you (or your organization) weren't flexible enough. Now think about your current campaign. What could go wrong? How could you flex to cope?

2. Think about 3 markets you have and describe the personalities of each as if they were a real, flesh-and-blood person. Now think about a market you're considering and describe it. Follow this process whenever you are preparing to enter a new market.

3. Recalling the Caterpillar story, what 5 steps can you take to defend your customer base against a sudden incursion by competitor from another country or region who decides to come play in your sandbox?

4. Now that you know your markets (the ones you described in Step 2), write down 3 tactics you could use in each market. For example, if you have an urban 18-25 market, one tactic might be to buy a list of cell phone numbers and text message them using shorthand slang.

5. Write down three ways in which you could guard against each of the following 5 killer mistakes:

   a. Being OK with losing customers.

   b. Not being courageous enough.

   c. Angering quickly or overreacting.

   d. Falling in love with your products.

   e. Drawing public critique.

121

ORIGINAL TEXT: Variation of Tactics

1. *Sun Tzu said: In war, the general receives his commands from the sovereign, collects his army and concentrates his forces*

2. *When in difficult country, do not encamp. In country where high roads intersect, join hands with your allies. Do not linger in dangerously isolated positions. In hemmed-in situations, you must resort to stratagem. In desperate position, you must fight.*

3. *There are roads which must not be followed, armies which must be not attacked, towns which must be besieged, positions which must not be contested, commands of the sovereign which must not be obeyed.*

4. *The general who thoroughly understands the advantages that accompany variation of tactics knows how to handle his troops.*

5. *The general who does not understand these, may be well acquainted with the configuration of the country, yet he will not be able to turn his knowledge to practical account.*

6. *So, the student of war who is unversed in the art of war of varying his plans, even though he be acquainted with the Five Advantages, will fail to make the best use of his men.*

7. Hence in the wise leader's plans, considerations of advantage and of disadvantage will be blended together.

8. If our expectation of advantage be tempered in this way, we may succeed in accomplishing the essential part of our schemes.

9. If, on the other hand, in the midst of difficulties we are always ready to seize an advantage, we may extricate ourselves from misfortune.

10. Reduce the hostile chiefs by inflicting damage on them; and make trouble for them, and keep them constantly engaged; hold out specious allurements, and make them rush to any given point.

11. The art of war teaches us to rely not on the likelihood of the enemy's not coming, but on our own readiness to receive him; not on the chance of his not attacking, but rather on the fact that we have made our position unassailable.

12. There are five dangerous faults which may affect a general:

   (1) Recklessness, which leads to destruction;

   (2) cowardice, which leads to capture;

   (3) a hasty temper, which can be provoked by insults;

   (4) a delicacy of honor which is sensitive to shame;

   (5) over-solicitude for his men, which exposes him to worry and trouble.

13. *These are the five besetting sins of a general, ruinous to the conduct of war.*

14. *When an army is overthrown and its leader slain, the cause will surely be found among these five dangerous faults. Let them be a subject of meditation.*

124

Chapter 11

LEADING YOUR ORGANIZATION IN PROFITABLE CAMPAIGNS— THE ARMY ON THE MARCH

W hen you enter into new marketing territory, you're taking your army on the march. You need to be able to read the signs and the terrain and react accordingly. The desired outcome would be to grab the high ground and control your customers and competitors perceptions.

In marketing, you must adapt to your customers. This means adjusting to their perceptions, tastes, likes and dislikes. Sun Tsu said, "Position yourself on the heights facing the sun. To win your battles, never attack uphill." Clearly, he favored getting the high ground.

Go for the gold in upscale markets

Sun Tsu's wisdom has meaning for upscale markets. To succeed, you need to price your products higher than your competitors. Upscale customers are keenly aware that they get what they pay for, and what they want to pay for is bigger, better, and blonder.

Don't try to compete on price in these markets, and don't go negative on the competition, especially if they're priced higher. That won't play on Rodeo Drive.

New marketing trends come along every season and most of them are pure hype. Let the competition spend the money to retool their campaigns, then take advantage of the distraction. Should the fad actually last for awhile, you can always jump into the middle of it once it's a proven winner. Bear in mind, though, that your sales figures won't be consistent...they'll drop off as the fad fades. Be prepared to ditch the fad.

If you have a choice between a trendy fad and a long-term trend, remember: the trend is your friend and the fad is bad.

Sun Tsu gives special advice for meeting the enemy in marshes. Marshes are unstable places, much like many 21st century markets. If your target market is unstable, grab that marketshare quickly and move on.

In big markets, change can happen in many different segments so stay flexible and ready to adapt. Be the high-quality product and keep one step ahead of your competitors by building a strong brand identity.

It's much easier to sell quality than price. Competing on price makes your product or service a commodity, and there's always someone who will sell for less—it's a losing game unless you're a very large corporation. Avoid the race to the bottom dollar by selling on quality.

Carve out your niche and brand your product to reflect high standards of quality. When you put out a quality image, your turnover will lessen because your people will be proud of that image.

Get higher prices by offering better value for the money

Train your sales staff on what to do when customers question your high price. It's very tempting for them to give into the customer by giving a discount, but it costs profits. Better to have a trained sales staff who can respectfully explain to the customer why your higher-priced product is the best value because of all the extra things that go into the product and service. Smart customers buy the best value, not the best price.

Common ploys customers use to complain about a price are:

- "Wow, you people sure are proud of your stuff."
- "Can you give me a discount?"
- "That's a lot of money for an XYZ."

Train your people to smile politely and counter with:

- "Well, actually, we're proud of the value we deliver to you. Let me tell you about all the extra features you get with this product that more than make up for the additional cost by saving you money in the long run…"

- "I'm sorry, we don't discount because we put our absolute best price on the product to start with, because it includes many extra features that…"

- "This XYZ is a lot of value for the money. Let me explain why…"

You get the idea—always counter a price objection with an explanation of everything the customer is getting for his money.

Stop the bleeding—dealing with bad press and mistakes

Sun Tsu warned against marching across flooded rivers until they subside. The 21st century marketing equivalent is a flood of bad news: scandal, a recall, an accident with a product. Stop your marketing when that happens. Try to use the press to your advantage. Be a superlative spin-doctor.

In a way, every market has some barriers to entry. You may have to have:

- Certain volumes
- Legal hassles
- Distribution issues
- Cost problems
- Education and training issues
- Cultural familiarity

When entering new markets, particularly if they have significant barriers that you must overcome, bring your team together and brainstorm to see if you've made any false assumptions, or if you are doing something out of habit or prejudice.

Here are a few of the more common false assumptions that Kim T. Gordon pointed out in the April 23, 2004 issue of entrepreneur.com:

1. You only have time to do marketing during slow times—Actually, you should make time to market all the time unless you want to live on an economic roller coaster.

2. Failure to focus—This is the death of many tech start-ups, who pursue too many projects that are all over the map.

128

3. Thinking you can get away without research and testing—You can't. You need market research to determine if there's sufficient market for your product. This will keep you from making expensive mistakes.

4. Sticking with just one or two tried-and-true marketing tactics—You just don't get exposure to the full range of potential customers when you only use one or two tricks.

5. Trying to go too cheap on marketing—If you don't bring in business, you won't survive. And most bankers require a marketing plan as part of your loan package.

6. Failing to maintain a professional image—Your marketing materials and business cards must be crisp and clean and your answering service or voicemail should be professional. Return calls within 24 hours—that's professional.

7. Neglecting current customers to market to new ones—It costs much less to market new products to a current customer than it does to a new customer.

8. Not using technology when it could help—Email management and contact management software are critical tools. Don't lose a valuable contact.

129

Keeping tabs on what the competition is up to

Defending against the competition starts with knowing what they're up to. If a particular competitor has a very strong position—i.e, a strong brand—he doesn't have to showboat and grandstand. Bear that in mind when you see quiet competitors.

If a competitor seems to be putting some distance between his product and you, or between him and you, watch out: he's planning to attack you. Be wary of Trojan horses. If a competitor has positioned himself or his product in a way that seems lame and it looks very easy for you to attack him, he's probably playing possum or has an ace in the hole. Don't fall for it.

Markets are like the sea. They might seem tranquil in one area for a little while, but that never lasts. Markets change, and sudden storms arise. Wise sailors watch the signs, and so should you.

Sun Tsu said, "When birds take flight, expect that the enemy is hiding there. When animals are startled, expect an ambush." In the 21st century, when you experience a sudden decline in sales, a competitor is probably undercutting you. Same thing for when your marketing consultants withdraw from you and don't have much to say—a competitor has gotten to them.

130

Here are a few other things to take note of:

- When a competitor is doing market research but says he's not really interested, don't believe him. He's about to launch a big campaign and he's covering his tracks.

- When they talk big but take no action, don't worry. They're throwing in the towel.

- When they start advertising in your market and making efforts to close the sale, watch out—they mean business.

- If they offer a truce and say they'll give back a market, it's one of two things: the market isn't worth a damn or they're going to back-stab you.

- They pull out of a campaign with their marketing team intact and together—watch out, they're just regrouping.

- They put some of their efforts into a market, but not all—watch out, you're being lured into spending resources on a dog market.

- They target a market but then don't do anything—they're at the end of a budget cycle and don't have sufficient resources.

- Their marketing people are doing collections—they're low on cash.

- They have a market right in front of them and they don't grab it—they're overwhelmed with other things.

When all the consultants start coming to you, your competitor has bailed. If a competitor asks you privately for info, he's really desperate...and confused. When you see unfocused sales staff, it means they don't respect their management.

A rapid shift in tone, message, or image means your competitor is deteriorating and they'll try anything. If their senior management seems edgy and short-tempered, they're overworked and stressed out.

When a campaign suddenly stops, someone ran out of cash. If they stop being nice and following the unwritten rules, they're desperate. When your competitor and his allies don't quite seem to be on the same page anymore, their alliance is falling apart.

If a competitor starts throwing in everything but the kitchen sink to make a deal work (like the "Zero Percent APR" car commercials of 2005 and 2006, just prior to the large GM and Ford lay-offs), they're having serious problems. Same thing for when he notches up his sales terms and wants invoices Net 10 days instead of Net 30 or 60.

Beware of competitors who storm into a market, grab a lot of market share, then pull out. What they're doing is gathering more resources to come back in even stronger, so they can dominate the market. Use that lull time to push your marketing every harder.

When your competitor approaches you about an alliance, he's either buying time to build his resources or you've truly got him on the ropes.

The most deadly thing to keep an eye out for, though, are competitors who look strong and solid, yet who don't jump into the market quickly. They maintain a presence in the market, but they don't go full-bore. They are biding their time as the build resources. Watch them.

132

When your distribution network isn't quite up to the task, you need to fix it. While you're fixing it, don't try to do new marketing. Just hold your ground and stay the course, like Caterpillar did.

Making those critical sales

New sales people are great, since they bring in fresh, new ideas. Unfortunately, they don't usually come with discipline. When you expand into new markets and add new sales people, make sure that you give them consistent messages so that they don't get confused. They need to know exactly what they're selling and how.

With markets you already have, you can lighten up and let your sales people bring you new sales ideas.

One of the ways in which you can make it easy for people to buy from you is by educating them. I've talked about educating them as to the value they get for their money, but if your product is technical in nature, you need to give customers a simple, clear explanation of why your product works and why it's superior.

Don't try to get too fancy with complicated explanations. If you do that, many customers' eyes will glaze over and your sales staff won't understand the product. Keep it simple. Think in terms of political sound-bites. Use a sound-bite of 30 seconds or less to explain how your product works in layman's terms. If your neighbor's 14-year-old kid understands what you say, you're golden.

We've gone through a lot of information in this chapter, but now you should have a better idea of how to fight the war that we call modern marketing. In particular, I've shown you how to handle upscale markets, how to justify higher prices through better value, and what to watch for with the competitions.

It gets even better in the next chapter, where you'll learn when to toot your horn and when to finesse a tough market. I'll show you how to navigate your army's campaign through all kinds of challenging terrain, all with the goal of increasing your bottom line.

Action Steps

1. Think back to an upscale market you campaigned in. Did your product have the highest price? Did you try to attack a higher-price competitor? Now think ahead to your next upscale market campaign. What could you do differently so that you profit more?

2. Consider a product that you've priced fairly high. Now make a list of five special features that make the product a good value for the money. Convey this information to your sales staff for use in countering price objections.

3. Think about a situation that you or a competitor faced when you got bad press or made a serious mistake in public. How was it coped with? Could that have been done better, using the press as a positive tool? How so?

4. Read back over the section on keeping tabs on the competition, and notice whether any of your current competitors are exhibiting those behaviors.

5. Ask one of your sales staff to explain to you exactly what your product is and what it does. If he or she isn't clear and concise—even worse, if they're confused—develop a simpler and clearer explanation.

ORIGINAL TEXT: The Army on the March

1. *Sun Tzu said: We come now to the question of encamping the army, and observing signs of the enemy. Pass quickly over mountains, and keep in the neighborhood of valleys.*

2. *Camp in high places, facing the sun. Do not climb heights in order to fight. So much for mountain warfare.*

3. *After crossing a river, you should get far away from it.*

4. *When an invading force crosses a river in its onward march, do not advance to meet it in mid-stream. It will be best to let half the army get across, and then deliver your attack.*

5. *If you are anxious to fight, you should not go to meet the invader near a river which he has to cross.*

6. *Moor your craft higher up than the enemy, and facing the sun. Do not move up-stream to meet the enemy. So much for river warfare.*

7. *In crossing salt-marshes, your sole concern should be to get over them quickly, without any delay.*

8. *If forced to fight in a salt-marsh, you should have water and grass near you, and get your back to a clump of trees. So much for operations in salt-marshes.*

9. *In dry, level country, take up an easily accessible position with rising ground to your right and on*

135

your rear, so that the danger may be in front, and safety lie behind. So much for campaigning in flat country.

10. *These are the four useful branches of military knowledge which enabled the Yellow Emperor to vanquish four several sovereigns.*

11. *All armies prefer high ground to low and sunny places to dark.*

12. *If you are careful of your men, and camp on hard ground, the army will be free from disease of every kind, and this will spell victory.*

13. *When you come to a hill or a bank, occupy the sunny side, with the slope on your right rear. Thus you will at once act for the benefit of your soldiers and utilize the natural advantages of the ground.*

14. *When, in consequence of heavy rains up-country, a river which you wish to ford is swollen and flecked with foam, you must wait until it subsides.*

15. *Country in which there are precipitous cliffs with torrents running between, deep natural hollows, confined places, tangled thickets, quagmires and crevasses, should be left with all possible speed and not approached.*

16. *While we keep away from such places, we should get the enemy to approach them; while we face them, we should let the enemy have them on his rear.*

17. *If in the neighborhood of your camp there should be any hilly country, ponds surrounded by aquatic grass, hollow basins filled with reeds, or woods with thick undergrowth, they must be carefully routed out and searched; for these are places where men in ambush or insidious spies are likely to be lurking.*

18. *When the enemy is close at hand and remains quiet, he is relying on the natural strength of his position.*

19. *When he keeps aloof and tries to provoke a battle, he is anxious for the other side to advance.*

20. *If his place of encampment is easy of access, he is tendering a bait.*

21. *Movement amongst the trees of a forest shows that the enemy is advancing. The appearance of a number of screens in the midst of thick grass means that the enemy wants to make us suspicious.*

22. *The rising of birds in their flight is the sign of an ambuscade. Startled beasts indicate that a sudden attack is coming.*

23. *When there is dust rising in a high column, it is the sign of chariots advancing; when the dust is low, but spread over a wide area, it betokens the approach of infantry. When it branches out in different directions, it shows that parties have been sent to collect firewood. A few clouds of dust moving to and fro signify that the army is encamping.*

137

24. Humble words and increased preparations are signs that the enemy is about to advance. Violent language and driving forward as if to the attack are signs that he will retreat.

25. When the light chariots come out first and take up a position on the wings, it is a sign that the enemy is forming for battle.

26. Peace proposals unaccompanied by a sworn covenant indicate a plot.

27. When there is much running about and the soldiers fall into rank, it means that the critical moment has come.

28. When some are seen advancing and some retreating, it is a lure.

29. When the soldiers stand leaning on their spears, they are faint from want of food.

30. If those who are sent to draw water begin by drinking themselves, the army is suffering from thirst.

31. If the enemy sees an advantage to be gained and makes no effort to secure it, the soldiers are exhausted.

32. If birds gather on any spot, it is unoccupied. Clamor by night betokens nervousness.

33. If there is disturbance in the camp, the general's authority is weak. If the banners and flags are shifted about, sedition is afoot. If the officers are angry, it means that the men are weary.

34. *When an army feeds its horses with grain and kills its cattle for food, and when the men do not hang their cooking-pots over the camp-fires, showing that they will not return to their tents, you may know that they are determined to fight to the death.*

35. *The sight of men whispering together in small knots or speaking in subdued tones points to disaffection amongst the rank and file.*

36. *Too frequent rewards signify that the enemy is at the end of his resources; too many punishments betray a condition of dire distress.*

37. *To begin by bluster, but afterwards to take fright at the enemy's numbers, shows a supreme lack of intelligence.*

38. *When envoys are sent with compliments in their mouths, it is a sign that the enemy wishes for a truce.*

39. *If the enemy's troops march up angrily and remain facing ours for a long time without either joining battle or taking themselves off again, the situation is one that demands great vigilance and circumspection.*

40. *If our troops are no more in number than the enemy, that is amply sufficient; it only means that no direct attack can be made. What we can do is simply to concentrate all our available strength, keep a close watch on the enemy, and obtain reinforcements.*

41. *He who exercises no forethought but makes light of his opponents is sure to be captured by them.*

42. If soldiers are punished before they have grown attached to you, they will not prove submissive; and, unless submissive, then will be practically useless. If, when the soldiers have become attached to you, punishments are not enforced, they will still be unless.

43. Therefore soldiers must be treated in the first instance with humanity, but kept under control by means of iron discipline. This is a certain road to victory.

44. If in training soldiers commands are habitually enforced, the army will be well-disciplined; if not, its discipline will be bad.

45. If a general shows confidence in his men but always insists on his orders being obeyed, the gain will be mutual.

140

Chapter 12

MARKET CONDITIONS—
CLASSIFICATION OF TERRAIN

———

I n the last chapter, you learned how to really get rockin' and rollin' when you're on the march with your army…also known as conducting a marketing campaign. But how do you read the signs of what the market is telling you? That's what I'm going to show you in this chapter, so read on…

Sun Tzu's army had to fight on plains, in woods, on his turf, on enemy turf, and in all kinds of weather. He said, "Some field positions are unobstructed, some are entangling, some are supporting, some are constricted, some give you a barricade, and some are spread out."

What's that mean for us? It means that…

- Some markets are wide open for the taking.

- Some markets can be dicey money-sucks.

- Some markets are yours—you dominate them.

- Others are tough.

- In some markets it's easy to protect your marketshare.

- In others it's tough to keep up brand identity.

Blow your horn when you win big in open markets

It's easy to get marketshare in wide open markets. What you must bear in mind is that it's easy for your competitors, too, since there are little or no barriers in an open market situation. Therefore, when you capture market share, let everybody and his brother know about it. Issue press releases, hold press conferences, and trumpet your glorious sales figures to the skies.

Success in open markets is a positive feedback loop—the more success you have, the more you will have if you keep publicizing your success. Stay in as long as you can for maximum profits.

Finessing the tricky markets

Tricky markets are ones that you can't get back into after you leave. You've got one shot at getting in and making sales, and if you blow it or you bail out, that's it. Dot-coms are particularly tricky markets.

Remember Webvan, the point-and-click-and-we'll-deliver-your-groceries people? And what about pets.com, with the cute sock monkey? Think anyone online would order from them again after they flopped? Nope. Online markets are very tricky. However, there is one notable exception: eToys. They're back in business after flopping in 2001.

Hold tight to what you've got

If you move out of a market in which you are entrenched, that's foolish. You've spent considerable resources to become entrenched, so stay there and keep on pulling in profits. The key is to realize when you're in an entrenched market.

Competitors will never admit that you're entrenched, because they want to pry you out of it. Don't fall for it. Stay where you're at. Likewise, if a competitor is entrenched and he doesn't realize it, you should try to lure him out so that you can positions yourself inside that nice, cozy trench. Foxholes are your friends.

Why it is vital to be first into a tough market

The best way to win a tough market is to be the first one in it. Once you've identified it as tough, do what you have to do to have speed. Get there first and grab as much market share as you can quickly before the competition shows up—and they will.

Now, if the competition gets in there first and grabs a ton of marketshare, don't blindly ape what they're doing. If you do that, you're just a "me-too." Instead, look for angles and segments that they have neglected and go after those.

Push your brand hard in an easy-to-protect market

Easy-to-protect markets are similar to wide-open ones. The discerning feature is that the customers are very loyal. Once they warm to you, you've got them. In these markets, get in there first and push your brand hard.

However, if the competition gets in there first, try to mess them up with disinformation and bad intelligence. Whatever you do, don't run a negative campaign…remember all those loyal customers? You will just look bad. Instead, try to mess with your competitor's head.

When it's tough to keep brand identity…

These markets just aren't all that profitable. When it's tough to keep brand identity, you are in what amounts to a commodities market. People are buying on price. Unless you're Wal-Mart,

Home Depot, or Toys 'R Us, you're probably not in the right arena. Find another market.

Matching your campaign and forces to the terrain

When you can't change the terrain, or market conditions, you must change your campaign and your people's behaviors. Make sure that your campaign isn't boring, ineffective, unfocused, disorganized, or lacking in focus. If it's any of those things and you can't change it, consider cutting your losses and starting from scratch with a whole new campaign.

Your branding might be a big hit with focus groups, but if it can be used against you, it needs retooling. If distribution had no problems but things just aren't selling, your campaign is boring. If it's the opposite, you're headed for a fall—get that distribution working.

When your sales people are pitching to anyone and everyone who will stand still for one second, your campaign lacks focus and that's not good. They should know their target market. Make it clear to them what they're selling and to whom, and how.

The terrain includes the competition, too. If they're putting out a strong message, you need to do the same. If they have diverse distribution channels, you won't be able to get by with one small, specialized distributor.

An alternative to going head-to-head is to just pick a different market when you're up against a strong message, diverse distribution channels and an aggressive marketing team.

Think like a Chinese general to win 21st century profits

A critical component of success for generals in Sun Tzu's time was a thorough knowledge of the enemy and the foresight to control battle conditions. You can't control the markets, but you can control what markets you enter, what markets you stay in and for how long, and how people perceive you.

Take a good hard look at your competitors. Where are they strong? Don't fight them there. Find out where they're weak, inexperienced, having problems, or just clueless. Attack them on those grounds.

For instance, if your competitor puts out an absolutely kick-ass product but customers complain about service, you need to transform your outfit into the service gurus. Remember Saturn? They found a weakness in the car-buying process and exploited it to the hilt.

It's worth your while to put in some time understanding your market and its rhythms. Knowing the market is your key to launching a successful campaign and knowing its rhythms means you'll launch at the right time. Move when there is opportunity.

145

Don't let ego cost you money

The worst reason in the world to launch a campaign is to keep up some sort of image, or because everyone else is doing it. If your current campaign is based on that, bail now. Businesses exist to make money, and the purpose of any marketing campaign is to sell. If your campaign isn't selling product, cut your losses.

Instead, devote some time to contemplating how to beat your competitors where they are weak. Also, think of how you can present your product so as to have maximum appeal to customers. Once you know your product, your competitors and your market, you can sell anything to anyone.

Whew, that was intense, wasn't it? But you've learned about the various types of markets and what to do when you find yourself in them, and that's invaluable.

In the next chapter, you'll learn some amazing tools for coping with typical situations that occur during campaigns. I'll show you how to maximize marketshare with flexibility, how to spin your image to the customer as a helpful partner, and what to do when you screw up during a campaign.

Action Steps

1. Think of a time when you were competing in an open market and you got in first. Did you tout your success openly? Now think ahead to future campaigns in open markets. After you get in first and succeed, how can you best publicize your success so that it feeds on itself?

2. Visualize a tricky market you've been in, one where you had one shot at success. Now think about future campaigns and target markets. Are any of them tricky? What can you do to maximize your effectiveness?

3. Are you entrenched in any markets right now? Are you getting messages from competitors to move on? Prepare a 10-minute speech to your sales staff on the importance of staying in that market.

4. Think of a competitor who's in an easy-to-protect market. What are 3 key pieces of disinformation you could put out to try to lure them out of that market?

5. Are you in any markets where your branding isn't working? Take a few moments and consider whether or not you're actually in a commodities market. If you are, make an exit strategy.

6. Consider 3 of your competitors. List each one's strengths, weaknesses, and vulnerabilities. List several ways in which you could take advantage of those weaknesses and vulnerabilities.

147

ORIGINAL TEXT: Classification of Terrain

1. *Sun Tzu said: We may distinguish six kinds of terrain, to wit: (1) Accessible ground; (2) entangling ground; (3) temporizing ground; (4) narrow passes; (5) precipitous heights; (6) positions at a great distance from the enemy.*

2. *Ground which can be freely traversed by both sides is called accessible.*

3. *With regard to ground of this nature, be before the enemy in occupying the raised and sunny spots, and carefully guard your line of supplies. Then you will be able to fight with advantage.*

4. *Ground which can be abandoned but is hard to re-occupy is called entangling.*

5. *From a position of this sort, if the enemy is unprepared, you may sally forth and defeat him. But if the enemy is prepared for your coming, and you fail to defeat him, then, return being impossible, disaster will ensue.*

6. *When the position is such that neither side will gain by making the first move, it is called temporizing ground.*

7. *In a position of this sort, even though the enemy should offer us an attractive bait, it will be advisable not to stir forth, but rather to retreat, thus enticing the enemy in his turn; then, when part of*

148

his army has come out, we may deliver our attack with advantage.

8. *With regard to narrow passes, if you can occupy them first, let them be strongly garrisoned and await the advent of the enemy.*

9. *Should the army forestall you in occupying a pass, do not go after him if the pass is fully garrisoned, but only if it is weakly garrisoned.*

10. *With regard to precipitous heights, if you are beforehand with your adversary, you should occupy the raised and sunny spots, and there wait for him to come up.*

11. *If the enemy has occupied them before you, do not follow him, but retreat and try to entice him away.*

12. *If you are situated at a great distance from the enemy, and the strength of the two armies is equal, it is not easy to provoke a battle, and fighting will be to your disadvantage.*

13. *These six are the principles connected with Earth. The general who has attained a responsible post must be careful to study them.*

14. *Now an army is exposed to six several calamities, not arising from natural causes, but from faults for which the general is responsible. These are: (1) Flight; (2) insubordination; (3) collapse; (4) ruin; (5) disorganization; (6) rout.*

15. *Other conditions being equal, if one force is hurled against another ten times its size, the result will be the flight of the former.*

16. *When the common soldiers are too strong and their officers too weak, the result is insubordination. When the officers are too strong and the common soldiers too weak, the result is collapse.*

17. *When the higher officers are angry and insubordinate, and on meeting the enemy give battle on their own account from a feeling of resentment, before the commander-in-chief can tell whether or no he is in a position to fight, the result is ruin.*

18. *When the general is weak and without authority; when his orders are not clear and distinct; when there are no fixes duties assigned to officers and men, and the ranks are formed in a slovenly haphazard manner, the result is utter disorganization.*

19. *When a general, unable to estimate the enemy's strength, allows an inferior force to engage a larger one, or hurls a weak detachment against a powerful one, and neglects to place picked soldiers in the front rank, the result must be rout.*

20. *These are six ways of courting defeat, which must be carefully noted by the general who has attained a responsible post.*

21. *The natural formation of the country is the soldier's best ally; but a power of estimating the adversary, of controlling the forces of victory, and of shrewdly*

calculating difficulties, dangers and distances, constitutes the test of a great general.

22. *He who knows these things, and in fighting puts his knowledge into practice, will win his battles. He who knows them not, nor practices them, will surely be defeated.*

23. *If fighting is sure to result in victory, then you must fight, even though the ruler forbid it; if fighting will not result in victory, then you must not fight even at the ruler's bidding.*

24. *The general who advances without coveting fame and retreats without fearing disgrace, whose only thought is to protect his country and do good service for his sovereign, is the jewel of the kingdom.*

25. *Regard your soldiers as your children, and they will follow you into the deepest valleys; look upon them as your own beloved sons, and they will stand by you even unto death.*

26. *If, however, you are indulgent, but unable to make your authority felt; kind-hearted, but unable to enforce your commands; and incapable, moreover, of quelling disorder: then your soldiers must be likened to spoilt children; they are useless for any practical purpose.*

27. *If we know that our own men are in a condition to attack, but are unaware that the enemy is not open to attack, we have gone only halfway towards victory.*

28. If we know that the enemy is open to attack, but are unaware that our own men are not in a condition to attack, we have gone only halfway towards victory.

29. If we know that the enemy is open to attack, and also know that our men are in a condition to attack, but are unaware that the nature of the ground makes fighting impracticable, we have still gone only halfway towards victory.

30. Hence the experienced soldier, once in motion, is never bewildered; once he has broken camp, he is never at a loss.

31. Hence the saying: If you know the enemy and know yourself, your victory will not stand in doubt; if you know Heaven and know Earth, you may make your victory complete.

Chapter 13

PICKING YOUR BATTLES— THE NINE SITUATIONS

Now that you've learned how to use your marketing army, and we've talked about different terrains, I'm going to share some extremely valuable information with you about the 9 different situations in which you can find yourself. Knowing these situations in advance can preserve your profits by saving you significant loss of marketshare, so read on…

Finding your footing in the 9 situations

If you've been around the marketing block a few times, you've probably had a déjà vu feeling of "been here, done this" during a few campaigns. Sun Tzu recognized that once his army penetrated enemy territory, the same sorts of situations, in the form of stages of a campaign, came up time and time again.

Being the smart guy that he was, Sun Tzu realized that these were recurring themes and he developed tactical responses to each.

The 9 types of situations or stages are:

- Tenuous—a new competitor comes into a market you're already in and you must defend your marketshare.

- Easy—you move into a new market with a new product. It isn't hard to make sales in this stage of the game.

- Scrappy—you must fight for every bit of marketshare you get, since everything's up for grabs.

- Open—no significant barriers to entry, so competitors can enter freely, as can you.

- Shared—similar companies are all in the same market, so the key is to form alliances and partnerships.

- Serious—you've spent considerable resources in this market, yet your competitors still hold significant market share.

- Difficult—there's a slow-down of some type. Some of your customers and distributors go out of business and you must cope.

- Limited—at this stage you are in transition and you rely on just a few resources stretched thin. Don't let the competition know you're running on a shoestring.

- Do-or-die—to win you have to go "all in", and commit all your resources. It's a "bet your company" decision.

Dodge the dangers of each situation

These situations are like markets—each has its own unique personality and quirks. And for each, you'll want to employ different tactics. Fortunately, Sun Tzu has done the heavy lifting for us.

When you're in a tenuous situation with a new competitor, tight up your campaign and don't leave any opportunity open. Mop it all up. An easy situation can actually be one of the hardest to manage, because there's a tendency to get complacent. Don't. Sell like there is no tomorrow.

In a scrappy situation, avoid competition by niching and branding your product to position it as well as possible. An open situation is a hyper-competitive animal, so you will have to compete hard.

When you find yourself in a shared situation, reach out to your competitors and for alliances. When it's a serious situation, focus on closing as many sales as possible.

In a difficult situation, your key to survival is to adapt—even rebrand, if need be. Hey, it worked for KFC… Limited situations are tough, but you will have to dig deep and make do. Beg, borrow, or steal until things improve.

Lastly, it should be self-evident that when you find yourself in a do-or-die situation, you'll have to slog it out and fight hard so that you are the winner, not the loser.

Keeping the competition off guard, Chinese-style

In the ancient Chinese world of war, success lay in a general's ability to use the enemy's strengths against him. This is still a fundamental principle of many modern martial arts.

Before you even begin your marketing, take a step towards ensuring success by locating the market segments in which your products stand the best chance of success. Do not try to sell ice to Eskimos just to show off your sales skills.

If you're up against larger competitors or an entrenched market, brand your product creatively so as to carve out a niche for yourself. Don't try to go head to head against the big dogs and eat out of their bowl. Instead, do a trick that earns you your own dog biscuit from the same customer.

Use anything you can against competitors. If they are…

- Big—make it about customization.

- Global—make it about personal service.

- Unskilled in an area—make that your showpiece segment.

- Developing a distribution channel—get in there and co-opt it.

When you've got the superior product on the market, do quality comparisons (remember the "Pepsi Challenge?" Pepsi consistently wins taste tests against Coke, so they've kept the Challenge through the years.) When you're big enough to compete on price, make it about not gouging customers.

Find a market segment that your competition just has to have to survive and attack with vigor. This is particularly effective if they are trying to enter one of your favorite markets, since this will force them to focus on their home base.

Sun Tzu said, "Avoid difficult situations. Attack the area where the enemy doesn't expect you." If a market is already very competitive, don't go in. Instead, go into a market where you're not expected.

Set up win-win situations

To survive long-term, take care of your people. By that I mean all of your people, not just marketing. Make sure your sales staff and your distributors all feel that they have a stake in your success. Reward them when you profit. When you cultivate loyalty like that, sales people and distributors will work with you even when times are hard because you've made them depend on you and your success.

Keep your distribution network as much under wraps as possible to avoid having it stolen or breached. Ask for total commitment from your marketing and sales staff and your distributors. That way, they'll be watching out for you.

Tired of hearing a bunch of griping about not being able to make deadlines? You need to go into "failure is not an option" mode. Find a way to put your people into a position so that they have no choice but to make the deadline. Then, watch them come through.

Maximize market share by being flexible

Twenty-first century markets move at warp speed. To thrive in them, you need to be able to do zero to sixty in a second or two and turn on a dime. Keep your instincts sharp and be ready to respond and problem-solve on the spot.

When the competition attacks your product for being new and different, attack them for being behind the curve and peddling old technology. If they attack you for being late to deliver, attack them on quality and attention to detail (something usually slips when you rush a product to market too fast.)

157

Always counter an attack with one of your own—never let stuff slide. Become known as a competitor who will fight back hard every time.

Position yourself as the customer's solution

The best way to sell to someone is to start by letting them know you hear their concerns. People want to be heard. When you listen and reflect their concerns, you make the important transformation from being just a company trying to put the hard sell on to a helpful friend who understands and is partnering with you to provide a solution.

This is precisely why you see IBM commercials touting "network solutions." IBM figured out that it was to their advantage to position themselves as a "solutions provider."

In your campaign, echo your customer's concerns and fears and address them. Position yourself as their helpful partner against whatever it is that's frustrating them. Control the message, but never reveal your plan.

Redefine the market, your product, and the focus if possible. Make it about your solutions. And do this craftily enough that your competitors never see it coming.

To lead the market, get your customers interested in what you're doing, hook them, then close the sale. Play on emotions.

Lifecycle of a campaign

Things always look easy in the beginning. There's market share to be had and none of the really ugly problems have cropped up yet. Nonetheless, this is the time to pour energy into your campaign and make sure that all of your people are fully committed. Problems will arise. Get things in place so that you can deal with them smoothly.

When your competitors come into the market, consider partnering with one or two of the better ones if it will lower your distribution costs and give you an advantage. Then, when things get tough during the limited stage, you won't have to operate totally on a shoestring.

Tenuous markets can occur at any time—you never know when a competitor might jump into your market, so cultivate customer loyalty while you can. Remember Caterpillar and Komatsu.

When it gets scrappy, throw obstacles in your competitors' way. Oil companies do this to each other all the time, usually through constriction of access to refining or shipping facilities. When it's a big open market, niche and brand like crazy to set yourself apart.

Empower your marketing team so that they can create success. Put them under the pressure of a tight deadline and they'll have to follow your lead. Take failure off the table as an option.

In Sun Tzu's day, it was critical for a general to know where the mountains, forests, ridges and reservoirs were located. He also had to enlist the aid of local guides. In the 21st century, you need to know your market and your customer's deep wants and needs.

What do you do when you screw up?

OK, it's great to apply Sun Tzu's principles, but we're all only human. We screw up sometimes. How do you recover?

It starts with attitude. Almost nothing is ever a total loss; you can almost always salvage something. And there's nothing so sweet as the taste of victory snatched from the brink of defeat. Be aware that you can survive a bad marketing stage, even customer loss. You can lose some ground and still recover. It's all in how you do it.

When a large competitor that you didn't see coming enters your sandbox, get in the way of any partnerships they might form. Take their ideas, steal their people, do what you need to do short of out-and-out illegal activity.

If you can pry one of his partners away and get them on your side, that's great. If not, then there are advantages to flying solo—you can change your strategy or products more quickly.

When you find an edge over the competition, hammer it for all it's worth. Make as much as you can out of it.

If customers start leaving a market, interview some of them and find out where they're taking their money. You'll probably uncover a new opportunity and you can get in there first.

Prevent screw-ups by doing things right from the beginning. Get everyone's buy-in and get rid of distractions. Total focus is what you want from your organization. Fight like hell to protect markets that are yours and keep out competitors.

When you launch into a new market, work fast, work smart, and work hard to build a loyal customer base and gain market-share quickly. Deploy your resources where they can gain you the biggest bang for the buck.

Marketing is like dating…you have to be committed for the long haul. When you see the competition turn away for a moment, make your move.

We've been through a lot of practical know-how in this chapter, but by now you should have a better feel for marketing situations or stages that can arise. Better yet, you know how to dodge problems, how to set up win-wins with your people, and how to position yourself as the customer's champion.

In the next chapter, we'll play with fire. I'll show you how to use it without getting burned. You'll see how to maximize your profits by uncovering customers' deepest desires and how to deliver what they truly need. Just turn the page, and I'll lay it all out for you…

Action Steps

1. In your current marketing campaign, which of the nine situations are you facing? In your last campaign, how many of the nine did you face and which ones were they?

2. How did you handle the situations in your last campaign? Now think of 3 ways to dodge the particular situation you are facing in your current campaign.

3. Think of an open market you're in or have been in. Figure out 5 ways in which you could keep the competition off guard.

4. Brainstorm about ways in which you can set up win-win situations for your people, including sales staff and distributors. Narrow it down to 3 viable ways.

5. In your previous campaign, think of an instance in which being flexible would have helped. Now consider your current campaign. How can you become more flexible?

6. Think of how your customers perceive you. Are you seen as a helpful partner who can be trusted to provide solutions, or just a seller? Now think of 5 messages you could use to come across as the customer's partner.

161

7. List three instances in which you or your organization has screwed up a campaign. How did you salvage things? Are there implications and applications for your current campaign?

ORIGINAL TEXT: The Nine Situations

1. *Sun Tzu said: The art of war recognizes nine varieties of ground: (1) Dispersive ground; (2) facile ground; (3) contentious ground; (4) open ground; (5) ground of intersecting highways; (6) serious ground; (7) difficult ground; (8) hemmed-in ground; (9) desperate ground.*

2. *When a chieftain is fighting in his own territory, it is dispersive ground.*

3. *When he has penetrated into hostile territory, but to no great distance, it is facile ground.*

4. *Ground the possession of which imports great advantage to either side, is contentious ground.*

5. *Ground on which each side has liberty of movement is open ground.*

6. *Ground which forms the key to three contiguous states, so that he who occupies it first has most of the Empire at his command, is a ground of intersecting highways.*

7. *When an army has penetrated into the heart of a hostile country, leaving a number of fortified cities in its rear, it is serious ground.*

8. *Mountain forests, rugged steeps, marshes and fens—all country that is hard to traverse: this is difficult ground.*

9. *Ground which is reached through narrow gorges, and from which we can only retire by tortuous paths, so that a small number of the enemy would suffice to crush a large body of our men: this is hemmed in ground.*

10. *Ground on which we can only be saved from destruction by fighting without delay, is desperate ground.*

11. *On dispersive ground, therefore, fight not. On facile ground, halt not. On contentious ground, attack not.*

12. *On open ground, do not try to block the enemy's way. On the ground of intersecting highways, join hands with your allies.*

13. *On serious ground, gather in plunder. In difficult ground, keep steadily on the march.*

14. *On hemmed-in ground, resort to stratagem. On desperate ground, fight.*

15. *Those who were called skillful leaders of old knew how to drive a wedge between the enemy's front and rear; to prevent co-operation between his large and small divisions; to hinder the good troops from rescuing the bad, the officers from rallying their men.*

16. *When the enemy's men were united, they managed to keep them in disorder.*

17. When it was to their advantage, they made a forward move; when otherwise, they stopped still.

18. If asked how to cope with a great host of the enemy in orderly array and on the point of marching to the attack, I should say: "Begin by seizing something which your opponent holds dear; then he will be amenable to your will."

19. Rapidity is the essence of war: take advantage of the enemy's unreadiness, make your way by unexpected routes, and attack unguarded spots.

20. The following are the principles to be observed by an invading force: The further you penetrate into a country, the greater will be the solidarity of your troops, and thus the defenders will not prevail against you.

21. Make forays in fertile country in order to supply your army with food.

22. Carefully study the well-being of your men, and do not overtax them. Concentrate your energy and hoard your strength. Keep your army continually on the move, and devise unfathomable plans.

23. Throw your soldiers into positions whence there is no escape, and they will prefer death to flight. If they will face death, there is nothing they may not achieve. Officers and men alike will put forth their uttermost strength.

24. Soldiers when in desperate straits lose the sense of fear. If there is no place of refuge, they will stand firm. If they are in hostile country, they will show a stubborn front. If there is no help for it, they will fight hard.

25. Thus, without waiting to be marshaled, the soldiers will be constantly on the qui vive; without waiting to be asked, they will do your will; without restrictions, they will be faithful; without giving orders, they can be trusted.

26. Prohibit the taking of omens, and do away with superstitious doubts. Then, until death itself comes, no calamity need be feared.

27. If our soldiers are not overburdened with money, it is not because they have a distaste for riches; if their lives are not unduly long, it is not because they are disinclined to longevity.

28. On the day they are ordered out to battle, your soldiers may weep, those sitting up bedewing their garments, and those lying down letting the tears run down their cheeks. But let them once be brought to bay, and they will display the courage of a Chu or a Kuei.

29. The skillful tactician may be likened to the shuai-jan. Now the shuai-jan is a snake that is found in the ChUng mountains. Strike at its head, and you will be attacked by its tail; strike at its tail, and you

will be attacked by its head; strike at its middle, and you will be attacked by head and tail both.

30. *Asked if an army can be made to imitate the shuai-jan, I should answer, Yes. For the men of Wu and the men of Yueh are enemies; yet if they are crossing a river in the same boat and are caught by a storm, they will come to each other's assistance just as the left hand helps the right.*

31. *Hence it is not enough to put one's trust in the tethering of horses, and the burying of chariot wheels in the ground*

32. *The principle on which to manage an army is to set up one standard of courage which all must reach.*

33. *How to make the best of both strong and weak—that is a question involving the proper use of ground.*

34. *Thus the skillful general conducts his army just as though he were leading a single man, willy-nilly, by the hand.*

35. *It is the business of a general to be quiet and thus ensure secrecy; upright and just, and thus maintain order.*

36. *He must be able to mystify his officers and men by false reports and appearances, and thus keep them in total ignorance.*

37. *By altering his arrangements and changing his plans, he keeps the enemy without definite knowledge. By*

shifting his camp and taking circuitous routes, he prevents the enemy from anticipating his purpose.

38. *At the critical moment, the leader of an army acts like one who has climbed up a height and then kicks away the ladder behind him. He carries his men deep into hostile territory before he shows his hand.*

39. *He burns his boats and breaks his cooking-pots; like a shepherd driving a flock of sheep, he drives his men this way and that, and nothing knows whither he is going.*

40. *To muster his host and bring it into danger:—this may be termed the business of the general.*

41. *The different measures suited to the nine varieties of ground; the expediency of aggressive or defensive tactics; and the fundamental laws of human nature: these are things that must most certainly be studied.*

42. *When invading hostile territory, the general principle is, that penetrating deeply brings cohesion; penetrating but a short way means dispersion.*

43. *When you leave your own country behind, and take your army across neighborhood territory, you find yourself on critical ground. When there are means of communication on all four sides, the ground is one of intersecting highways.*

44. *When you penetrate deeply into a country, it is serious ground. When you penetrate but a little way, it is facile ground.*

45. *When you have the enemy's strongholds on your rear, and narrow passes in front, it is hemmed-in ground. When there is no place of refuge at all, it is desperate ground.*

46. *Therefore, on dispersive ground, I would inspire my men with unity of purpose. On facile ground, I would see that there is close connection between all parts of my army.*

47. *On contentious ground, I would hurry up my rear.*

48. *On open ground, I would keep a vigilant eye on my defenses. On ground of intersecting highways, I would consolidate my alliances.*

49. *On serious ground, I would try to ensure a continuous stream of supplies. On difficult ground, I would keep pushing on along the road.*

50. *On hemmed-in ground, I would block any way of retreat. On desperate ground, I would proclaim to my soldiers the hopelessness of saving their lives.*

51. *For it is the soldier's disposition to offer an obstinate resistance when surrounded, to fight hard when he cannot help himself, and to obey promptly when he has fallen into danger.*

52. *We cannot enter into alliance with neighboring princes until we are acquainted with their designs. We are not fit to lead an army on the march unless we are familiar with the face of the country—its*

mountains and forests, its pitfalls and precipices, its marshes and swamps. We shall be unable to turn natural advantages to account unless we make use of local guides.

53. To be ignored of any one of the following four or five principles does not befit a warlike prince.

54. When a warlike prince attacks a powerful state, his generalship shows itself in preventing the concentration of the enemy's forces. He overawes his opponents, and their allies are prevented from joining against him.

55. Hence he does not strive to ally himself with all and sundry, nor does he foster the power of other states. He carries out his own secret designs, keeping his antagonists in awe. Thus he is able to capture their cities and overthrow their kingdoms.

56. Bestow rewards without regard to rule, issue orders without regard to previous arrangements; and you will be able to handle a whole army as though you had to do with but a single man.

57. Confront your soldiers with the deed itself; never let them know your design. When the outlook is bright, bring it before their eyes; but tell them nothing when the situation is gloomy.

58. Place your army in deadly peril, and it will survive; plunge it into desperate straits, and it will come off in safety.

59. *For it is precisely when a force has fallen into harm's way that is capable of striking a blow for victory.*

60. *Success in warfare is gained by carefully accommodating ourselves to the enemy's purpose.*

61. *By persistently hanging on the enemy's flank, we shall succeed in the long run in killing the commander-in-chief.*

62. *This is called ability to accomplish a thing by sheer cunning.*

63. *On the day that you take up your command, block the frontier passes, destroy the official tallies, and stop the passage of all emissaries.*

64. *Be stern in the council-chamber, so that you may control the situation.*

65. *If the enemy leaves a door open, you must rush in.*

66. *Forestall your opponent by seizing what he holds dear, and subtly contrive to time his arrival on the ground.*

67. *Walk in the path defined by rule, and accommodate yourself to the enemy until you can fight a decisive battle.*

68. *At first, then, exhibit the coyness of a maiden, until the enemy gives you an opening; afterwards emulate the rapidity of a running hare, and it will be too late for the enemy to oppose you.*

171

Chapter 14

DISRUPTING THE COMPETITION—ATTACK BY FIRE

I n the last chapter, you learned how to recognize situations that arise frequently. Now we're going to take it to the next level—burning down your competitor's house. Not literally, of course, but with pretty much the same effect…

Give customers what they need when they need it

The 21st century marketing equivalent of fire is the customers' burning desires. If you've read about Maslow's hierarchy of human needs, it's similar to the needs of customers. Most customer needs fall into five basic categories:

- The need to feel secure and safe—this one increased greatly after September 11th, 2001.

- The need to feel comforted and nurtured—this is an extension of a basic childhood need, and explains comfort foods.

- The need for status, recognition and prestige—this is why the awards and trophies industry exists.

- The need to get or gain something—this is basic greed.

- The need for love, approval and affection—this is why car ads always show sexy women.

Once you understand your target market's deepest desires, you can cater to them by branding and positioning your product as the fulfillment of their needs. Timing plays a key role—customers don't always have the same needs.

In late November and for most of December, most customers are in a festive, free-spending mood and their primary need is for Christmas presents so that they can be good givers. Customers also spend the most on liquor and party supplies during this season.

In January, everything changes. Instead of needing to celebrate and be the good host, customers needs shift to losing weight, getting in shape, and getting back to business. In February, there's a big push to show love on Valentine's Day. In the summer, there's a frenzy of needs—the need to buy or sell a new home, the need to look good on the beach, and the need to take a vacation.

Make sure your timing is appropriate to the season of the customers' needs.

Play to customers desires for maximum profits

If you can play your customer's desires like a violin, you can make sweet music all the way to the bank. What you have to realize is that the competition is also trying to target their marketing towards customer's desires, so your best bet is to uncover a desire that's gone unnoticed.

Remember the car cup-holder example I mentioned earlier? That's a prime example of uncovering a desire that went unnoticed...the car companies knew that people wanted reliable transportation, but failed to pick up on the fact that people also wanted to be able to drink coffee or sodas while driving.

When you zero in on an overlooked desire, design your campaign so that you build on the customer's frustration that he can't get what he wants. Let the desire build, then unleash the product. Don't wait too long—timing is critical.

If the unnoticed desire that you're catering to goes against prevailing attitudes, tread carefully. You don't want to spit into the wind, or as Sun Tsu put it, "Don't attack into the wind." And in 21st century America, you certainly don't want to offend anyone.

Often the real desire that motivates a customer to buy a product has nothing to do with the product's function. Sleek sports cars, for instance, are not generally bought purely for their performance. They're bought to satisfy the customer's need for prestige and approval from others. In particular, middle-aged men going through a mid-life crisis are notorious for buying red convertible sports cars to try to hang onto their youth.

Look for desires that aren't visible. They may be desires that people aren't exactly proud of, such as greed or lust…maybe even the desire to get out of doing work. People don't come out and share these desires with you, so you will have to work to uncover them.

A prime example of concealed desires is the existence of cookie-dough ice cream. Eating raw cookie dough gives many people a feeling of comfort, since their mother always allowed them to lick the spoons when she made cookies. But as adults, it's frowned on to eat raw cookie dough. Then the ice cream companies caught onto that desire and packaged it as an ice cream flavor, thus lending an air of respectability to it.

175

Why you must check your emotions at the door

Emotions have a placed in marketing—during brainstorming. But in the actual strategy and execution, it's best to use your brain. Don't let your pride or anger ruin a perfectly profitable campaign.

Watch out for getting your buttons pushed. That can cause you to react emotionally when you should have thought thing through. Don't let your ego drive campaigns. Never feel like you have to go into a market just to "show them." ("Them" being the competition.)

Periodically analyze calmly whether or not you should be in a market, and if not, cut your losses and get out of it. Emotions can always change. A campaign that was fun can quit being fun, yet still be profitable—stay in. And a fun campaign can be a loser, profit-wise. In that case, get out.

Sun Tsu said, "A nation once destroyed cannot be brought back to life. Dead men do not return to the living." What he's saying to you is that once you lose a sale, it's gone. That applies double to customers—once you lose one, he's gone forever.

And when you lose a customer, you lose seven potential customers, because that's how many people the average dissatisfied customer tells about his bad experience. Sadly, the average satisfied customer only tells one other person.

This why you need to keep your emotions in check. Productivity and sales stem from great strategy.

Learned a lot? I thought so. Now you know how to play with fire without getting burned. Just give customers what they really want, take the time to find out their deepest desires, and keep your emotions under control and you'll profit handsomely.

In the next chapter, I'll show you how to deploy your spies effectively. Don't worry, I'm not talking about full-scale industrial espionage…I'm talking about market research and luring competitors people away whenever possible. When you've got intel on your market and your competitors, it's like shining a light into a dark room.

Action Steps

1. Think about your target market and three of your current products. What customer need are you satisfying with these products? Does your marketing reflect that need, touching on it in many ways, or are you marketing to a different need? List three ways in which your current campaign could better tap into a customer need that your product satisfies.

2. List 5 desires that your target market has, preferable desires that relate to your product. Does your campaign reflect those? If not, retool your message so that you play to desires.

3. Recall three instances in which your emotions got the better of you. Now write down a different strategy you could have used to cope with the situation.

177

ORIGINAL TEXT: Attack by Fire

1. *Sun Tzu said: There are five ways of attacking with fire. The first is to burn soldiers in their camp; the second is to burn stores; the third is to burn baggage trains; the fourth is to burn arsenals and magazines; the fifth is to hurl dropping fire amongst the enemy.*

2. *In order to carry out an attack, we must have means available. The material for raising fire should always be kept in readiness.*

3. *There is a proper season for making attacks with fire, and special days for starting a conflagration.*

4. *The proper season is when the weather is very dry; the special days are those when the moon is in the constellations of the Sieve, the Wall, the Wing or the Cross-bar; for these four are all days of rising wind.*

5. *In attacking with fire, one should be prepared to meet five possible developments:*

6. *(1) When fire breaks out inside to enemy's camp, respond at once with an attack from without.*

7. *(2) If there is an outbreak of fire, but the enemy's soldiers remain quiet, bide your time and do not attack.*

8. *(3) When the force of the flames has reached its height, follow it up with an attack, if that is practicable; if not, stay where you are.*

9. *(4) If it is possible to make an assault with fire from without, do not wait for it to break out within, but deliver your attack at a favorable moment.*

10. *(5) When you start a fire, be to windward of it. Do not attack from the leeward.*

11. *A wind that rises in the daytime lasts long, but a night breeze soon falls.*

12. *In every army, the five developments connected with fire must be known, the movements of the stars calculated, and a watch kept for the proper days.*

13. *Hence those who use fire as an aid to the attack show intelligence; those who use water as an aid to the attack gain an accession of strength.*

14. *By means of water, an enemy may be intercepted, but not robbed of all his belongings.*

15. *Unhappy is the fate of one who tries to win his battles and succeed in his attacks without cultivating the spirit of enterprise; for the result is waste of time and general stagnation.*

16. *Hence the saying: The enlightened ruler lays his plans well ahead; the good general cultivates his resources.*

17. *Move not unless you see an advantage; use not your troops unless there is something to be gained; fight not unless the position is critical.*

18. No ruler should put troops into the field merely to gratify his own spleen; no general should fight a battle simply out of pique.

19. If it is to your advantage, make a forward move; if not, stay where you are.

20. Anger may in time change to gladness; vexation may be succeeded by content.

21. But a kingdom that has once been destroyed can never come again into being; nor can the dead ever be brought back to life.

22. Hence the enlightened ruler is heedful, and the good general full of caution. This is the way to keep a country at peace and an army intact.

180

Chapter 15

FOCUS GROUPS AND NETWORKING—USE OF SPIES

D on't blush—spies are essential. We live in the information age. Even in Sun Tzu's time, information was vital. Ancient Chinese armies made use of numerous spies. Our 21st century equivalent is focus groups, networking, and other market research.

Campaigns cost a lot of money. When a campaign brings in huge sales, it's called a good investment. When it flops, it's called a waste and you might be called "fired." What makes the difference? Good information.

Sun Tzu realized that there were five different types of military intelligence and information sources, and they are all very adaptable to the modern world of marketing.

Getting the biggest bang for your marketing research bucks

Running campaigns takes serious cash and resources. It's as expensive as running an army. Sun Tzu had that in mind when he said, "All successful armies require thousands of men…and every day, a large amount of money must be spent."

Yes, marketing costs money. You may as well make that clear from the very beginning to your senior management. But when

181

you do, make sure you position marketing not as a cost but as an investment in future sales. Leaders have a knee-jerk reaction to costs—they don't like them. But they are always looking for good investments.

People have a lot of demands for their attention today. To market effectively, you have to develop a laser-like focus for your campaign. For instance, if you were to pay for a banner ad on a popular website, where would you have it placed?

If you'd done your market research, you'd know that when people pull up a site, their eyes are drawn first to the upper left-hand corner of the screen. People are also drawn to color, and banners that feature a person in them do particularly well since they have a humanizing effect on cyberspace.

A well-thought-out marketing plan that takes current market segment conditions and attitudes into account will save money by making sales efficiently. Thus, it is worth it to invest in market research.

Success with spies

Sun Tzu said, "You need local spies. Get them by hiring people from the countryside." The 21st century equivalent is marketing research. While I don't recommend you hire just anyone from the countryside, I do strongly suggest that you pay for professional research on your target market. To neglect to do so is to commit the marketing equivalent of shooting in the dark...and that wastes bullets.

Spies also come in the form of competitor's people who may be disgruntled and looking to jump ship. Always keep the lines of communication open so that such people can contact you.

When you do hire a competitor's man or woman away from them, treat them like gold and encourage them to spread the word to the competitor's current people that you have many wonderful opportunities for them.

Same thing goes for distributors—find out who the competition is using and do what you need to do to sway them over to you.

Reverse engineering is another form of spying, and it's completely legal. Buy one of your competitor's products and give it to your engineers so that they can figure out how it works. Then bring in your manufacturing people and find a way to produce it cheaper. This is what many Japanese companies excel in doing—reverse-engineering American products and producing them at less cost.

Take the time to look for any weaknesses or flaws in your competitor's product. Then exploit them as much as you can by making your product overcome those weaknesses.

183

Disinformation campaigns can be very profitable. This involves planting false information about your next moves so that your competitors hear about it and respond to it. Then, you make your real move once they've been thrown off track.

Protect your valuable assets

Be very good to your research and development people— consider the cost if they were to become unhappy and go over to your competitor. That would be a disaster. Better to treat them well so you don't lose them.

When someone brings you confidential information on a competitor, act as if it is the most natural thing in the world, and reward them handsomely. You want to encourage this behavior so that you can gain more information.

Pay attention to patterns in your competitor's strategy and take advantage of them. Do they always launch their Christmas sales campaign the day after Thanksgiving? Then launch yours two days before Thanksgiving, before people leave for the holiday.

In any good army, intelligence is key. That goes for companies, too. Sure, you'd like to attack your competitor's product and grab his customers and distributors. But to do so, you need to know how his product works, how his customers think, and how his distributors operate.

Where does your competitor get his market research? Steal those people or pay for the info.

Be careful, though. People often take it personally when you steal their people and distributors. Stay in the shadows and cover your tracks. Don't make a habit of it—instead, steal strategically, where it will do you the most good. A competitor's shipping clerk isn't nearly as useful to you as one of his marketing managers.

It's not enough to learn from your mistakes. You must also learn from your successes—and it's a hell of a lot more fun.

To be the best, hire the best. Don't be afraid to hire people smarter than you. Then use them to gather information.

Action Steps

1. Think of your current campaign. Are you getting the maximum bang for your buck? Think of 5 ways in which you could spend your marketing dollars to better advantage.

2. Write down three people you know who either work for a competitor or who used to work for a competitor. Now ask each for three referrals of people who currently work for a competitor and ask them to make the first contact. Try to steal them.

3. How do you reward people who bring you valuable information? Think of 5 ways you could reward such people, get the necessary rewards so you'll have them handy and start implementing a reward system.

ORIGINAL TEXT: Use of Spies

1. Sun Tzu said: Raising a host of a hundred thousand men and marching them great distances entails heavy loss on the people and a drain on the resources of the State. The daily expenditure will amount to a thousand ounces of silver. There will be commotion at home and abroad, and men will drop down exhausted on the highways. As many as seven hundred thousand families will be impeded in their labor.

2. Hostile armies may face each other for years, striving for the victory which is decided in a single day. This being so, to remain in ignorance of the enemy's condition simply because one grudges the outlay of a hundred ounces of silver in honors and emoluments, is the height of inhumanity.

3. One who acts thus is no leader of men, no present help to his sovereign, no master of victory.

4. Thus, what enables the wise sovereign and the good general to strike and conquer, and achieve things beyond the reach of ordinary men, is foreknowledge.

5. Now this foreknowledge cannot be elicited from spirits; it cannot be obtained inductively from experience, nor by any deductive calculation.

6. Knowledge of the enemy's dispositions can only be obtained from other men.

7. Hence the use of spies, of whom there are five classes: (1) Local spies; (2) inward spies; (3) converted spies; (4) doomed spies; (5) surviving spies.

8. When these five kinds of spy are all at work, none can discover the secret system. This is called "divine manipulation of the threads." It is the sovereign's most precious faculty.

9. Having local spies means employing the services of the inhabitants of a district.

10. Having inward spies, making use of officials of the enemy.

11. Having converted spies, getting hold of the enemy's spies and using them for our own purposes.

12. Having doomed spies, doing certain things openly for purposes of deception, and allowing our spies to know of them and report them to the enemy.

13. Surviving spies, finally, are those who bring back news from the enemy's camp.

14. Hence it is that which none in the whole army are more intimate relations to be maintained than with spies. None should be more liberally rewarded. In no other business should greater secrecy be preserved.

15. Spies cannot be usefully employed without a certain intuitive sagacity.

16. They cannot be properly managed without benevolence and straightforwardness.

17. *Without subtle ingenuity of mind, one cannot make certain of the truth of their reports.*

18. *Be subtle! be subtle! and use your spies for every kind of business.*

19. *If a secret piece of news is divulged by a spy before the time is ripe, he must be put to death together with the man to whom the secret was told.*

20. *Whether the object be to crush an army, to storm a city, or to assassinate an individual, it is always necessary to begin by finding out the names of the attendants, the aides-de-camp, and door-keepers and sentries of the general in command. Our spies must be commissioned to ascertain these.*

21. *The enemy's spies who have come to spy on us must be sought out, tempted with bribes, led away and comfortably housed. Thus they will become converted spies and available for our service.*

22. *It is through the information brought by the converted spy that we are able to acquire and employ local and inward spies.*

23. *It is owing to his information, again, that we can cause the doomed spy to carry false tidings to the enemy.*

24. *Lastly, it is by his information that the surviving spy can be used on appointed occasions.*

25. *The end and aim of spying in all its five varieties is knowledge of the enemy; and this knowledge can only be derived, in the first instance, from the converted spy. Hence it is essential that the converted spy be treated with the utmost liberality.*

26. *Of old, the rise of the Yin dynasty was due to I Chih who had served under the Hsia. Likewise, the rise of the Chou dynasty was due to Lu Ya who had served under the Yin.*

27. *Hence it is only the enlightened ruler and the wise general who will use the highest intelligence of the army for purposes of spying and thereby they achieve great results. Spies are a most important element in water, because on them depends an army's ability to move.*

189

Chapter 16

SUMMARY

B y now I hope you've learned and internalized some of the major messages of Sun Tzu's teachings as they apply to 21st century leadership and marketing.

One of the key concepts that I continue to find the most useful is to do the unexpected things. Be as unpredictable as you can. Better yet, stick with a pattern of behavior for a short while, just long enough to lure your competitors into thinking they can predict your next campaign…then do something totally new.

Another core concept is to avoid head-to-head conflict, particularly with the same weapons. Head-to-head conflict only works if you are the stronger competitor, like Pepsi in the Pepsi Challenge Taste Tests.

Instead of going head-to-head, find the enemy's weakness and exploit it. Find the spot where they are not and invade. Locate a lapse in their timing and strike then. When you win, follow through. Don't be like the guys in the horror movies that leave the monster alive…because then they will come back for revenge. Crush your opponents until they're dead.

When you capture a market, don't get complacent. Remember what happened to AT&T when they took customers for granted. Shift to defense, and you'll be more like Caterpillar— able to fend off any possible incursions by competitors like Komatsu.

To run a successful campaign, do your market research first. Then set the goals. Set an agenda so that you get the results you want. Remember that campaigns have a shelf-life and that things change quickly these days.

Whenever possible, feed off of your competitor's campaigns and energies. It's free money. Make sure that your people know that when you win, they win, so that they feel invested in your success.

To win, take the necessary steps to rule out failure. Make sure your people know that their only route to success lies in your success.

Listen carefully to focus groups and avoid the temptation to make it one big ego-stroke. Hear what they're saying.

Find ways to offer better value and you can raise your price point. Look for opportunities to launch sneak attacks and leverage them fully. Talk to customers and find out what needs they have that are not being fulfilled, then go for it.

Sell to customers where they are, don't make them travel too far to you. Partner with distributors and producers so that they profit from your successes. Make them bleed when you bleed, and feast when you feast.

Every problem is a veiled opportunity—you just have to look hard. Keep your emotions out of business decisions. When you misstep, spin it to your advantage.

Now that you recognize types of markets and situations, use that knowledge to make strategic moves at just the right times. Brand and position your products to take advantage of shifting demographics and don't hesitate to rebrand if necessary—it worked for KFC.

Always see your products from the customer's point of view—what's in it for them? Sell the benefits, not the features. The customer's ultimate goal isn't a quarter-inch drill, it's quarter-inch holes. Sell those quarter-inch holes.

Use market research and people who come to you from a competitor as spies. Reward people handsomely for competitive information, and protect those people.

If you can master the valuable information I've shared with you, you can become a superb Samurai of 21st century leadership and marketing.

HOW TO CLAIM YOUR FREE
BONUSES ON THE COVER

As a special thank-you gift for purchasing *The Art of War for the New Millennium*, I have included an exclusive package of bonuses, which retail for $467.00.

FREE Bonus Gift #1: The Single Greatest Marketing Secret You Can Use To Build Your Business™ (CD#1, retail value $199.00 value)

FREE Bonus Gift #2: The Greatest Success Secret In The World™ (CD#2, retail value $199.00 value)

FREE Bonus Gift #3: How Ordinary People Make Extraordinary Money On The Internet™ (CD#3, retail value $69.00 value)

All you have to do to get your bonus gifts is visit my special website at:

artofwar.websiteconversionexpert.com
(without the http://www)

ABOUT THE AUTHOR

"Who The Heck Is Dan Lok And Why Is Everyone Talking About Him?"

A former college dropout, Dan Lok transformed himself from a grocery bagger in a local supermarket to a multi-millionaire. Dan came to North America with little knowledge of the English language and few contacts. Today, Dan is one of the most sought-after business mentors on the Web, as well as a best-selling author. His reputation includes his title as the World's #1 Website Conversion Expert.

Dan's unique mixture of real-world experience and stunning financial success have earned him a spot among the most trusted experts alive. The "best in biz" actively seek out Dan's knowledge, advice and expertise on all matters related to marketing, despite his obnoxious, "pull no punches" attitude. In fact, his attitude is what makes him so appealing. Dan is the very definition of cutting edge, helping those he mentors as well as aspiring entrepreneurs realize what's working (and what's not working) on the Web.

His company, Quick Turn Marketing International, Ltd., produce what many consider to be the finest educational programs ever in Internet marketing and wealth creation. These materials enable clients to achieve financial freedom, to live the life they've always wanted, and to build a secure future for their family – tomorrow and for years to come.

Dan is also the author of *Forbidden Psychological Tactics and Creativity Sucks.*

Dan enjoys martial arts, swimming and skiing. He reads a couple of books a week and loves movies and great restaurants. (Just in case you want to send him a present!)

To find out what Dan is up to now, visit him at:

www.WebsiteConversionExpert.com